Contents

PAGE 56

PAGE 62

PAGE 75

PAGE 6

FICTION

My Weekly Annual 2010

PAGE 82

PAGE 136

Printed and Published in Great Britain by D C Thomson & Co. Ltd., 185 Fleet Street, London EC4A 2HS. © D C Thomson & Co. Ltd., 2009. While every reasonable care will be taken, neither D C Thomson & Co. Ltd., nor its agents accept liability for loss or damage to colour transparencies or any other material submitted to this publication.

By best-selling novelist

Marian Keyes

. . . .

Precious

You'll love this lively tale by the Queen of Chick-Lit!
Prepare to laugh out loud…

H e was the most beautiful man I'd ever seen.

Granted, I was only twenty, and not much of a judge, but all the same.

I was three weeks into my first "proper" job and I'd just come back from the bar after a frustrating attempt to buy a post-work round of drinks. Not only had it taken for ever to get served but then the barman had seemed disinclined to believe I was over eighteen.

That's how young I was – desperate to look older.

I banged a glass in front of Teresa and another one in front of my chair and I blazed indignantly, "If they went any slower, they'd be taking drinks back from people and refunding them their money!"

He laughed and I fell silent. Where had he come from? This creature with his gorgeous dark wavy hair and skin so pale it almost had a bluish hue.

My colleague and, as it happens, new best friend – you bond quickly at that age – Teresa, introduced us. "Orla, this is my friend Bryan."

Suddenly Bryan, second only to Nigel in the pantheon of dorky boy names, blossomed into something violently romantic.

He was small and slight, but not boyish. More like a fully grown man who'd been reduced by, say, 20 per cent. And the thin wrists that stuck out beneath his white cuffs were covered with fine black hair.

I was desperate to look older

I was convinced he was foreign, perhaps of Russian ancestry. No Irish man could be so elegant and delicate. But when I mumblingly asked him what nationality he was, he sounded surprised and said, "Irish."

Was he sure, I pressed.

Quite sure, he said. His mother was from Limerick, one of the Limerick McNamaras and his father's family had lived in Meath since time immemorial.

The next day at work, Teresa delivered the news that almost caused me to levitate. "Bryan likes you." To my dumb, idiotic face she expanded, "He was asking all about you, you know."

Eventually I released the question which tormented me. "Have you ever, you know… with him?" "Bryan?" She laughed a laugh I didn't understand. "Nah, he's a bit too –" another laugh, "–
Continued overleaf…

Continued from previous page

mysterious for me."

I wasn't inclined to believe her. How could she not want him? How could anyone not want him?

That night we all went out again. This was when I discovered I was taller than him.

His movements mesmerised me. He did everything – lit cigarettes, fiddled with his glass – with a hard, easy grace. Next to him I was a lumpish peasant and my coarse unworthiness rendered me mute.

"Are you all right?" Teresa's voice was innocently surprised. "It's just that normally you're so … lively."

"Fine," I insisted, a sickly smile nailed to my face.

He looked as if he'd spent his childhood as a pale face at a bedroom window, watching sadly while the other cruder, more robust children rough-housed with each other on the grass. But it turned out that he'd been very good at football.

When he wasn't answering questions, he was a man of few words. He didn't bother with small talk, which impressed me no end and served to silence me further.

"I wonder…" he said at one stage. "I wonder what it's like to be a loofah."

"Yeah, I wonder…" I tried to make my voice sound musing, although until that very moment I hadn't entertained an atom of curiosity about the inner workings

of a loofah. "Scratchy, I suppose."

"Scratchy!" He acted as if I'd said something profound and I nearly burst with pride – and relief.

Being kissed by him was like being pelted with marshmallows and I was so grateful that he wanted me.

But my inadequacy burgeoned. He was just too beautiful, too perfect, too refined, too self-contained. Then I discovered I was six months older than him. It made me worse. I somehow felt like a horny-handed, meaty pervert who was taking advantage of him.

Waiting for him to discover that I wouldn't do became unbearable, so I hastened it myself. I watched his exasperation grow with my awkward, giggly silences. It was like seeing an out-of-control truck speed down a hill, directly towards me. I was powerless to stop it and powerless to get out of the way.

Every night when he dropped me home I swore to myself that next time – if I was lucky enough to get a next time – it would be different. I'd talk, I'd laugh, I'd make him laugh. But when the next time came, my words would disappear on me and we'd end up kissing more out of needing something to do.

From the beginning I'd known he was moving to New York and that the most I would ever get with him was a couple of months. Even while I fantasised about his staying for me, I knew he wouldn't.

So he went, just as expected.

wasn't around any more.

Teresa wouldn't let me be heartbroken. "I like him," she said, "he's my friend, after all, but isn't he a bit precious?"

For a long, long time I thought calling someone 'precious' was actually a compliment.

Perhaps six months after he'd left, news filtered back from New York that he was going out with a new woman – a painter. When I'd recovered from the initial kick-in-the-stomach shock, I thought: oh, but of course. A painter, a tormented artist. What else?

I could see her. Neurotic and sexy, with an elusive, quicksilver quality which held Bryan in her thrall. She was tiny – she'd have to be, to be worthy of him. Skinny with childlike buttocks, but nothing childlike about her sexuality.

She never ate, she subsisted on

"There was this bloke when I was twenty. I never got over him…"

The only jarring note was that he was going to work for a bank.

And I never got over him. Sometimes I used to say it. I liked the sound of it. "There was this bloke when I was twenty and I suppose…" brave smile, deep breath "… I never got over him."

It was actually a relief when he was gone. I was sick and crazy, but it was easier to deal with when he

cigarettes and black coffee. She dressed entirely in black, her black polo-neck covered with paint stains which she never noticed. Sometimes she deliberately cut herself with the scalpel she used on her canvasses. While the rest of the world slept, she prowled around her loft, flinging paint at canvas and exclaiming with **Continued overleaf…**

Continued from previous page
insomniac despair. I scorned my own regular seven-hour slumbers – how stolid, and how embarrassingly stable.

Time passed and I went out with other men, and did my very best to let them break my heart. Some of them made quite a good stab at it for the wedding, bringing Danielle, his wife with him.

From the moment I heard they were coming, I became clenched and oxygen-deprived with waiting. You'd swear it was I who was getting married.

The morning of the wedding I spent a long, long time on my

Then I saw him. Patiently I waited to see if I'd fall in a faint or break into a sweat

too, but not enough to wipe out his memory completely.

"I'm sorry," I said more than once. "You see there was this bloke when I was twenty and I…" brave smile, deep breath, "…never got over him."

Most of them bought it. Some were quite sympathetic, some were hurt, some angry and one of them told me I had an overactive imagination and that I'd want to cop on to myself.

The day I heard he was marrying the neurotic, insomniac painter, I thought I took the news quite well. Until I was on the bus on the way home and, with a sweaty rush of hot and cold, realised that if I didn't get off at the next stop, there was a good chance I'd vomit.

And somehow it was ten years since he'd left Ireland, Teresa was getting married, and Bryan was coming home from New York

appearance, prepared to embrace any small setback – a chip in my nail varnish, a missing earring – as a major disaster.

I didn't see them in the church, but when we got to the hotel and saw the seating plan, I couldn't decide if I was glad or appalled to find I was at the same table as them. But my friend, Jennifer was also at the same table, she'd provide a buffer.

I was twisted up, tight as a walnut, my eyes working the reception room. Then I saw him. Patiently I waited to see if I'd fall in a faint or break out into a sweat or rush to vomit. Nothing happened.

At the same time he saw me and came towards me, as my heart knocked ever louder echoes into my ears. We smiled and our greeting was the height of politeness, apart from the fact that he had forgotten my name. *Still 'not quite of this world'*, I thought.

Then I focused on the woman next to him. I'd seen her already: she was impossible to miss. She didn't look the way I expected Bryan's wife to look. For a start she was tall, taller than him. About my height, actually. And her hair was bright yellow. Not exactly blonde, more like the Day-Glo dazzle of yellow Opal Fruits. Glorious.

Her dress was also yellow, but not quite the same shade. How brave, I thought, suddenly angry

with my own tweely co-ordinated look. She wore lots of red lipgloss, as if she'd fallen into a patch of raspberry jam. And I was surprised that she didn't look as if she subsisted on just cigarettes and coffee. One or two square meals got past those raspberry-jam lips. I could see no obvious scalpel scars on her bare arms, either.

"How's New York?" I asked him.

"Fine," he said.

"Good," I said, "I was worried about it, you know."

No, I didn't actually say it, but I thought it. To be fair, I didn't exactly set the conversation alight either. Even ten years on he could deprive me of the power of speech.

During the meal she was very loud and drank a lot. Tossing back the yellow hair that didn't quite go with her yellow dress, she seemed to like Jennifer. During one break in conversation she confided loudly into Jennifer's face that her cellulite was so bad she could see Calista Flockhart's profile in it.

As I discreetly checked beneath the table for scars on her legs, I couldn't help but notice that her legs were quite hairy. For a second this didn't fit with my picture of her, then it all made sense. She was a free spirit, thumbing her nose at convention. My respect for her went through the roof and I felt ashamed of my own smooth, waxed legs. I was nothing but an **Continued overleaf...**

Continued from previous page
unimaginative slave.

After the speeches, all the smokers stampeded out to the lawn. En route, Jennifer got me in a headlock. "Heavens, that Bryan is so boring! Getting conversation out of him is like trying to get blood out of a turnip. Where's Al? I need a light."

Al was my escort, my "plus one". Actually he was the man who'd told me that I had an overactive imagination and that I'd want to cop on to myself.

"She's a house painter, a lairy painter and decorator. She's drunk and lairy and awful."

A house painter. Not a picture painter, a house painter. Of course it was a shock. Until I began to process it. How cool was that? A woman in a man's world, confounding expectations, bucking the trend …

Abruptly, I stopped. That was enough. As if on cue, across the room came Al, homing straight at me, looking so happy to see me,

"You know that Danielle? She's just tried to start a fight with me in the ladies"

I'd grown quite attached to him. I liked his plain-spokenness. The fact that he spoke at all was very attractive, I suddenly acknowledged, as I eyed Bryan across the table and realised conversation would be non-existent until one of the smokers returned.

Time dragged, then next thing Jennifer catapulted at high speed across the room towards me.

"You know that Danielle?" Her voice had a tremble. "She's just tried to start a fight with me in the ladies. Lairy piece of work."

"Well, she's an artist." I shrugged. "They're temperamental."

"What are you talking about?" Jennifer asked. "She's a painter."

"Yeah, an artist."

"No," she corrected impatiently.

even though he'd only been gone ten minutes. I began walking towards him.

Lairy, I said to myself. I liked that word. *Lairy*, I repeated. *Lairy*.

Marian Keyes

For Beginners...

Queen of chick-lit!

She was born in 1963
"I was a month overdue and often wonder what my life would have been like if I'd been born on time and been a dynamic, sunny Leo, instead of a perfectionist Virgo."

She was raised in Dublin then spent her twenties in London
"I did a law degree, then put it to good use by going to London and getting a job as a waitress. Eventually I got a job in an accounts office. I thought I'd be there forever."

Her first book *Watermelon* was published in Ireland in 1995
"I began writing stories four months before I finally stopped drinking, (Keyes gave up alcohol 15 years ago), and sent them to a publisher, claiming I'd written part of a novel. Which I hadn't. They said – send the novel, and for once in my self-destructive life I didn't shoot myself in the foot. I wrote four chapters in a week, and was offered a three book contract."

Her books have been translated into 32 different languages, such as Hebrew and Japanese. And that's about it!
"To sum up, I used to be addicted to shoes, handbags and chocolate in all its wonderful forms. I've given up the chocolate and I'm learning to cook proper food. All quite normal, really!"

To sum up, I used to be addicted to shoes, handbags and chocolate!

PICTURE: PENGUIN BOOKS

"Hello,

You'll be inspired by this touching story that looks with hope to the future, not the past

By Kathleen Wilkinson

The weekend away in the Lake District had been booked six months ago. Jo managed to change the family room to a twin one but yet, she felt reluctant to go. There was still so much to do at home with moving to another house. Jo didn't feel ready for it and yet Emma's six years were passing by so quickly. What difference could a weekend away make?

Stepping out into the spring air, they left behind the confines of the small hotel and ambled along the country lane for a morning stroll.

"Mummy?"

"Mmm?" Jo took in the view of the green fields on her right, up to the woods and the rolling green hills beyond.

"Why do I have to wear a jacket? The sun's out." Emma pulled down her zip. "I'm too hot."

"It'll be raining soon," Jo replied still looking at the hills in the distance and the clouds.

Daffodils!

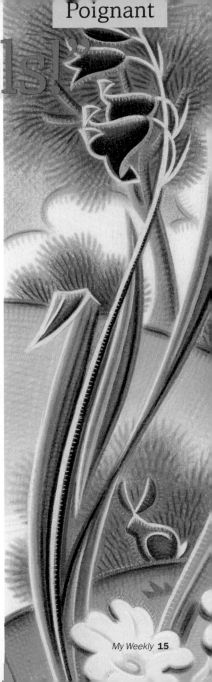

"I can wear it when it rains." Emma took off her jacket and handed it to Jo.

"Mummy?"

"Mmm?"

"That's not right, Mummy. We're told not to say 'mmm' at school. You should say 'yes'."

"Sorry, darling. Yes?"

"Why do we have hills?"

"Because we do."

"Mummy? Why doesn't Daddy love you any more?" she asked, looking so innocent.

"We've already talked about this, sweetheart."

Jo looked ahead to the village and beyond. "Mummy?"

"What?"

"Do you still love Daddy?"

"Can you stop saying 'Mummy' all the time? Just say what you've got to say."

"You're grumpy!"

"I'm not!"

"Yes, you are!"

"No, I'm…" Jo took a deep breath. "No, I'm not, really. Let's walk to the lake and throw stones."

"Yeah, let's see who can throw farther," she said excitely.

"Farthest," Jo corrected.

"Yeah, like we did before, on holiday… where was it?"

Continued overleaf…

Continued from previous page

"Where was what, darling?"

"Mummy, you're not listening!"

"Sorry. What did you say?"

"Doesn't matter." Emma kicked a stone with her wellington boot.

Jo and Emma wandered through the village past the petrol station and a row of shops including a small newsagent's.

"Can I have some sweets?"

"Let's see who throws the farthest. If it's you, then you can have some sweets and if it's me… well…"

"Yes?"

"I'll think about it!"

"Oh, Mu-ummy!" Emma whined.

They walked on past the tourist shops and restaurants, the hotels and church and the garden centre until there were no shops left. Taking a turning off the road by the boats for hire, Emma ran slightly ahead towards the lake. It started to drizzle.

"Jacket on, Emma! Hurry, it's starting to rain," called Jo.

Emma skipped back to put on her lemon-coloured jacket. "Can we still throw stones in the lake, Mummy, can we? Please!"

"Yes, if we get in the shelter of those trees up ahead, we can."

They hurried towards the scattering of trees on the bend of the lake. Emma shook off her hood and whispered, "Do you think there are any bears?"

"Shall we look?" Jo whispered back, joining in the game.

Emma fixed her mummy with huge brown eyes and shook her head slowly before suddenly changing her mind.

"Yes, let's do that."

Emma took Jo's hand and they walked farther into the wood and around the bend in the lake.

"Look, Mummy! Look at all the daffodils! Aren't they lovely?"

"It's like a lake of flowers."

"There must be ten million hundred, twenty billion and ten!" Emma laughed and ran towards them, then skipped into them. "Hello, daffodils!" she shouted.

The drizzle stopped. Emma ran all the way down to the lake.

"Careful, Emma, not so far," Jo called. "Wait for Mummy, darling."

Jo caught up and they stood together, beneath the trees by the edge of the water. A cool breeze blew off the lake.

"Look, Mummy! Look how they all dance and sway in the breeze!"

Emma picked a daffodil, held it up between her fingers and studied it.

"She's got a yellow funnel!" exclaimed Emma.

"Maybe that's how she talks to the other flowers," suggested Jo.

Emma giggled. "Maybe she SHOUTS, like me! HELLO DAFFODILS!" The flower moved in the breeze. "Now she's bowing up and down. I've never seen so many daffodils! Can we get some to take home?"

"Good idea, we'll buy some later."

"Oh!" Emma looked intently up to the sky for a few seconds and sighed. "Mummy?"

"Mmm. Yes, darling."

"Do you see that wispy cloud up there? The one all by itself?"

"Yes."

"Do you think it's lonely?" Jo

"HELLO DAFFODILS!" Emma shrieked as the golden flowers danced in the breeze

"Promise?"

"Promise." Just then sunshine fell on all the flowers. "Look! The raindrops are sparkling like diamonds!" Emma's face shone.

She smiled at her mummy. Jo slipped a daffodil in her daughter's buttonhole, took out her mobile phone and captured the sheer joy of the moment.

"You look just like a princess with all her dancing yellow fairies."

"Don't be silly, Mummy." Emma put down the daffodil. "OK, let's see who can throw farther."

"Farthest," corrected Jo again.

They skimmed the water with their stones. Jo looked beyond the lake, her thoughts drifting.

"Mummy? How many skims did you get?"

"I counted five, Em."

"No, you didn't, you only got three! What are you listening for, Mummy?" Emma asked.

"I'm sorry, love, it's nothing. I was just lost in my own thoughts."

looked from the cloud to Emma before feeling the first drops of rain on her face.

Back at the hotel that evening, Jo tucked Emma up in bed. A pretty pot of daffodils sat on the bedside table.

"I'm going to plant these in the garden when I get home," Emma said. "They're excited about it as well, you know Mummy."

"Are they? How do you know?"

"Do you know what they told me?" Emma whispered.

"No, what did they say?" Jo whispered back. "Tell me."

"They told me winter is over."

Jo stared pensively at the bright yellow flowers.

"And it is, isn't it, Mummy?"

Jo became engrossed in her own thoughts as she gazed at the field of daffodils and beyond.

A few moments passed.

"Yes, you're right, it is over. All **Continued overleaf...**

Continued from previous page

over," she said slowly. She took Emma's hand and said, "We had such a lovely afternoon, didn't we? Spring time has shown me a lot today. The daffodils were so… alive! And I think it's catching…"

Emma nodded.

"You asked about Daddy this morning… I did love him once but about to have another happy picture in my head."

"Really?"

"Yes, of you sound asleep in your bed!" Jo kissed Emma lightly on the cheek.

Emma yawned. "Are the daffodils going to sleep now too, do you think, Mummy?"

"They certainly are."

"Mummy," little Emma asked, "why doesn't Daddy love you any more?"

now… well, like winter… it is all over." Gently she rubbed her little daughter's hand. "The daffodils are right. It's time to let spring in through our door."

"You mean our garden!"

Jo laughed. "I suppose I do, sweetheart! And we've got all those flowers we bought to plant in our new garden."

"Can I help?" Emma beamed.

"'Course you can. We'll do it together, shall we?"

"I can still see the daffodils swaying and dancing when I close my eyes. Can you, Mummy?"

Jo closed her eyes. "Yes, I can. Sometimes it's almost like a film and sometimes just a picture. And do you know what?"

"No?"

"We're going to make lots of new pictures together, for in here." Jo pointed to her eyes.

Emma laughed. "And now, I'm

"'Night, 'night, daffodils, 'night, 'night, Mummy, love you."

"And I love you too." Tenderly, Jo watched Emma as she closed her eyes. Looking at the daffodils in the pot, she touched them gently as if to say "goodnight".

As she glanced back at her daughter on tip-toeing out of the room, Jo knew the past had finally gone but it had also opened up hope for the future.

She was determined it would be a bright and happy future for both of them. And the weekend had only just begun.

ABOUT THE AUTHOR

Kathleen is presently studying for a Diploma in Creative Writing at the University of Hull and writes for a community newsletter

Pretty As A Picture

You'll feel a shiver of dread when you reach the end of our chilling story…

By Teresa Hewitt

Entranced, Marion stared at the painting. She saw a green lawn before a great grey house and, in the foreground, a small girl in Victorian dress. She had one hand on a wooden hoop, pink ribbons in her hair, and sparkling dark eyes which locked with Marion's as if sharing a mischievous secret.

To Marion she seemed more alive, more real, than any of the people bustling about in the auction-room. The picture was titled *Claudia at Play*.

An elderly woman, stooped and faded, stepped up beside Marion and asked, "Do you like her?"

"Oh, I do," Marion breathed, still enchanted by the painting.

"I can see she likes you, too," the old lady said, urgent and intense. "Take my advice, turn around and leave. Walk away and never think about this painting again."

She hadn't been thinking about buying it actually. There was no room in her cottage for such a thing and it would look out of place. But the little girl's face was enchanting and her bold black eyes seemed to follow Marion with amusement, with invitation.

"You'll regret it. That painting is evil," the old lady said, and in her eyes Marion read a real sorrow, deep and intense. "Once she has you she won't let you go."

Moira was silent. What could she say to such madness? She turned to look at the painting again, and when she turned back the woman was no longer there.

"I *will* buy you," Marion said to herself, looking into Claudia's eyes, and the little girl laughed back.

When *Claudia at Play* came under the auctioneer's hammer Marion was the only bidder and she got it at its starting price of £200. She felt a thrill of excitment as she signed her cheque and collected the painting.

"Is anything known about its history?" Marion asked the auctioneer's assistant.

He finished taping brown paper over the protective padding. "It's not a famous work. Painted by a family member, possibly; it wasn't displayed in the gallery but found in the attic." He handed her the bulky package. "Still, fashions change. You could find it has some value, if you hang onto it. And it has a very nice frame."

"I didn't buy it to make a profit," Marion said. "I just liked it – it spoke to me!"

Her eyes had lost their sparkle and now seemed to gleam malevolently

He smiled. "I would say that's the very best reason for buying a painting, if you ask me!"

Back at her cottage Marion unpacked her picture and hung it in her little passageway. It looked very well there, snuggled in between the beams. Claudia looked down at Marion laughing, you could even fancy triumphant.

"You like it here, don't you?" Marion said aloud.

At that moment Marion's cat Beadle appeared. He stopped, one paw lifted – it was comical, the way he seemed to be appraising the new arrival, the outrage in his stiffened pose – and then he ran, streaking away suddenly in a whirl of hissing, spitting fur through the cat flap in the front door.

Marion laughed. "I know it's not a Rembrandt – but really!"

She straightened the painting one last time, smiled again at her Claudia, and went to light a fire in the tiny sitting room; it seemed to have suddenly become very cold and the cheery glow would be more than welcome.

It did get a little lonely here at nighttime but Marion was used to that and later, as she got up to go to bed, the little sound she heard didn't alarm her – it was probably Beadle returning from his nightly mouse-hunt.

She popped her head out into the passage. No cat but her painting had slipped sideways.

"Now, now," she teased, straightening it. "Time to settle down, there's a good girl!"

The painting looked… different in this low light. Claudia's eyes had lost their happy sparkle and instead seemed to gleam rather malevolently. Her smile blazed out just the same but now made the child look quite unpleasant.

"I'll move you tomorrow, my lady," Marion said aloud. "We'll find you a brighter spot!"

As she climbed the stairs the urge to turn and look at the painting was almost irresistible but somehow she reached her bedroom without giving in. It was quite ridiculous, feeling so uneasy at the thought of the child's eyes **Continued overleaf…**

Continued from previous page
following her up the stairs.

She left the door ajar for Beadle – he often curled up on her bed in the night and she liked his comforting warmth.

Morning came and Marion had had a restless night; the cottage had seemed more creaky than usual, the wind intensely mournful, and her dreams had been disturbing, though she couldn't remember them now. At one time she had been convinced there was someone standing beside the bed looking down at her, someone who wished her harm, but when she opened her eyes with a pounding heart the room was empty, the moonlight streaming in and the only sound an owl's screech piercing the night.

She went down to the kitchen and found Mrs Canning there already, washing up.

"Have you seen Beadle?" Marion asked. "He didn't come in for his supper."

"Haven't looked," the woman replied shortly. "Been too busy tidying up! Party going on last night, was there?"

Marion decided it was best not to reply – Mrs Canning was prone to a good grumble – and asked instead, "Have you seen my new painting yet? What do you think of the new family member, then?"

Mrs Canning froze, her back straight as a ramrod. "I saw it, yes. Couldn't stand it myself, but it's your house after all."

Really, the woman was positively rude sometimes! Marion left her to it and went out to the hall, intending to look for Beadle.

In the passage, the painting was lying face down on the flagstones.

"Oh!" Marion stooped to pick it up before marching back to confront Mrs Canning.

"Even though you may not like it, I'd rather you didn't move it," she finished coldly. "It's old and rather fragile."

Mrs Canning sniffed, hanging up her tea towel. "I didn't. I wouldn't touch it for love nor money and that's the truth. Something nasty

about it, if you ask me."

After Mrs Canning left, Marion found she didn't much like the atmosphere in the cottage today. It seemed too quiet, almost menacing with its dark corners and lurking shadows. But she was not a fanciful woman, and she quickly shook the feelings off. A walk down to the village would clear her head of nonsense and the vague, distant terrors of the night.

She came back bearing fresh bread and cheese. The trip had certainly done her good; she was feeling brisk and positive as she passed through her gate and – ah! – there was Beadle…

Marion's caught her breath as she saw him. The cat looked terrified, his ears pressed flat to his head, his lips drawn back in a snarl.

"Beadle!" She bent down and scooped him up with a hand under his belly and felt the little creature's heart beating, thrumming wildly against her fingertips. His fur was dark and wet, and what was this…?

Beadle's collar had a soaked pink ribbon tied around it. Marion knew immediately what must have happened: the village children had grabbed him for their games, dressing him up, pushing him around in a pram, perhaps. Marion remembered doing something of the sort herself as a child. They had probably meant no harm. But Beadle wasn't used to children; no

There was someone beside her bed, someone who wished her harm

wonder the poor mite was terrified.

An old nursery rhyme began floating around in her head – ding-dong bell, pussy's in the well…

"Poor boy," Marion soothed, and she pushed the door open with one hand. "Have your dinner and curl up by the fire –"

As soon as the door to the dark passage swung open, Beadle shot out of her hands and streaked away as fast as he could down the path and out of sight.

"My goodness," Marion said aloud. "Whatever's the matter with him?" but she wasn't going to chase after him now and she stepped across the threshold. Immediately the dark, cool silence of the cottage settled around her. She looked down the long, narrow passage and remembered: Claudia.

The strangest thought came to her that perhaps Beadle was afraid to come in because he didn't want to pass the painting.

Continued overleaf…

Continued from previous page

It was simply a ridiculous thought, and yet at this very moment Marion was experiencing the strangest reluctance to walk by Claudia herself.

"Nonsense," she told herself briskly, "You're going peculiar in your old age, lady!"

There had been two bows yesterday in Claudia's hair, one each side, catching back the flowing dark tresses. Now there was one, only one, and she had just seen the other in a place it could not possibly be, not unless she was going mad – on Beadle's collar!

Her hand flew to her heart,

There had been two bows in Claudia's hair – now there was only one!

She walked up to the picture and faced it. And there was, she saw with relief, nothing frightening about it at all. It was simply a painting of green lawns and blue sky and Claudia, hand on her hoop, smiling out at her.

No malevolence, as indeed Marion had known deep in her sensible heart there could not be. The girl looked just mischievous, as children do, her black eyes sparkling with a lively delight.

"Well, there you go," Marion said aloud. "Silly old cat! Silly old woman, too," and she smiled at Claudia, lightheaded with relief. Nothing but a pretty little girl with bows in her hair and…

Marion's head snapped up and her heart thudded sickly with shock. She stared and stared at the painting and then she ran on shaking legs into the kitchen, every nerve tingling with a terror so great she felt ill.

fluttering like a trapped bird. Even though she could hardly breathe she reached for the phone.

A n ordinary painting," David said. "Not an undiscovered Constable but you didn't waste your money," he smiled at her. "It's an attractive thing so you'll certainly be able to sell it on."

Marion took a hearty sip of the brandy he had poured her.

"I don't care about the money, David, but you think I'm imagining things, don't you?"

David hesitated. "Well… your feelings were very real," he said, carefully. "I've never seen you in such a state! Being too scared even to walk past the picture! You can see now you were being a bit of a silly goose, can't you, Marion dear?" His eyes held hers, a little teasing, a little anxious. "It's just a painting – look at it!"

Marion forced herself to glance

at the picture he had removed from the wall and laid on the kitchen table. She knew that David was right. It looked like any other painting; Claudia smiled up, blank and harmless and un-alive.

"I do feel silly now," she confessed. "But the ribbon on Beadle's collar – I know I didn't imagine that!"

"I'm sure you didn't," David said. "But you do see now that it can't possibly be the ribbon from the picture. Did she come to life and step down out of the frame and go out at night and fix it on his collar? I don't think so!" He was laughing at her now, kind and friendly, and she joined in, just a little uneasy. "See, it sounds absurd now I've said it aloud, doesn't it? Your nerves were rattled and you put

two and two together and made an impossible five. She never had two ribbons in the first place."

Marion stared at the painting. She had been so sure…

"I suppose that must be it," she said slowly. "It does seem daft now I'm thinking straight again. Oh dear, I've been a ridiculous old fool, haven't I?"

"Of course not," David said. "Imagination can play strange tricks on the mind, you know. Alone all night in this lonely spot – you just gave yourself a very bad fright, my dear!"

"I know one thing. I don't want it in the house any more, and I'll be taking it down to the charity shop this afternoon. Unless you could take it with you?"

"Can't, I'm afraid," David said, apologetically, indicating his bicycle clips. "But if it makes you feel better – I'll put it in the shed. You needn't even look at it again. Just pop her in the car and drive her away to her new home."

Marion felt shaky after her troubled night and the fright of the morning, so she had a light lunch and washed up her plate, her fingers so nervous and clumsy that she knocked her bracelet off the draining board and down behind the sink. But that could wait. Everything could wait. Her house would soon be hers again, her safe **Continued overleaf…**

and friendly haven.

Still no sign of Beadle, but she had a feeling he would come back just as soon as her task was done. She opened the shed door and grabbed the painting, bundled it into the boot of her car and slammed it shut.

"There!" she said aloud. "You're off, my girl. Outstayed your welcome, I'm afraid."

The woman in the charity shop was delighted. "Well!" she said, taking Claudia, "Isn't this a lovely picture?"

"Yes, I thought so…" Marion said hesitantly.

"Are you sure you want to give it away? It looks as if it could be somewhat valuable."

"Yes, indeed, I'm quite sure," Marion said firmly.

"Such a pretty little girl," the woman said, smiling down with a look that was almost fond. Marion knew exactly what she was seeing and what her next words would be.

"I might even buy it myself."

"Why don't you?" Marion said eagerly. She would feel better, so much better, if Claudia found a new mistress, tonight. "I'd like her to go to a good home and I've been told the frame itself is worth a bit."

"You know, I think I will have her! She's looking at me just as if she's asking me to," and she spoke to Claudia with fond reproach,

"Naughty little minx, aren't you?"

On her way out, at the last moment, Marion couldn't resist it. Almost against her will her head turned slowly and her eyes darted to the picture the woman had set against the wall. She dared to look into Claudia's face one more time.

Claudia's laughing black eyes, sparkled with wickedness and her right hand gripped the frame of her painted hoop. But Marion was horrified to see that on her slender wrist was a bracelet that was never there before.

Marion knew at once it was hers, the one she had lost down the back of the kitchen sink this morning.

She turned and fled from the shop, feeling lighter and happier with every yard she put between herself and Claudia.

Her house would soon be hers again, her safe and friendly haven

She felt safe that tonight Claudia would hang on someone else's wall, haunt their dreams, and play her nasty little tricks elsewhere. Marion had had a narrow escape but it was all over now.

When she got home Mrs Canning's bicycle was already at the cottage gate when Marion went into the kitchen – oh, the relief to pass that empty space upon the wall! – where Mrs Canning was on her hands and knees, polishing the flagstones.

"Have you seen Beadle around?"

"No, but you had a phone call whilst you was out."

"David, I expect?" Dear David, checking up on her.

"No, it was a young girl," Mrs Canning continued, scrubbing away fiercely. "The line was bad."

Marion stared at Mrs Canning as she set her bag down, numbly, on the kitchen table.

"She said she had something of yours, something you lost," the woman went on. "But not to worry, she said, she'll be bringing it back to you tonight."

"Are you sure she asked for me?" Marion said, her voice barely a whisper. "Not a wrong number?"

Mrs Canning lifted her head and looked right at her, hearing the strange note of panic. Goodness, her employer looked terrified as she began to pace around the room, looking frantically from one window to another. Spent too much time alone that was her trouble, filling her head with silly imaginings. You'd think she'd be glad to know someone had found her bracelet. She squeezed out the cloth and got to her feet.

"'Twas only a young girl," she said. "Nothing to get yourself in a state about. Just a child."

"Did she give her name?" Marion asked, though the words were torn out of her, waiting on Mrs Canning's answer as if her life depended on it.

But even before Mrs Canning opened her mouth and spoke the name she knew what it would be as her mind flashed back to a prophecy, spoken on a day that seemed a lifetime ago: Once she has you, she'll never let you go…

Always At

Sometimes the greatest words of wisdom come from the most unexpected source as this moving story illustrates

By Isobel Stewart

Time doesn't really heal, but it does help.

It's three years ago since Peter died, and I remember people saying that to me – not right away, but later.

Needless to say, I didn't believe them, but I know now the passing of weeks, months, years, does help.

I can do things now that I couldn't do at first. I can pay bills, I can change plugs, I can even change a tyre. But these are small things, practical things. There are lots more important ways that I can see time helping.

I can look at my wedding photo without that treacherous tightness in my throat. I can wake up knowing that Peter isn't there any more, that he won't ever be there again, and I can handle that.

I can smile, I can laugh, where I once felt I would never be able to do either of these things again.

And most of all, I can talk to Jack about his father. We smile when we remember things that happened when Jack was very small.

Peter's impatience for Jack to start speaking, and his delight and astonishment when Jack, sitting in his high chair at nearly two, held out his plate to Peter, and demanded, "More, Daddy."

Memories like sweeping up the fallen leaves into Jack's little truck, and the bonfire we had later. The early Christmases we shared. And the summer Peter taught Jack to swim at the big pool near us.

When Jack finally mastered a few strokes on his own, Peter was so proud that he lost his balance and fell in. The time when Jack was helping Peter to bath Rusty, in the big basin out in the garden, and Rusty managed to overturn the

My Side

They went everywhere together

basin, and Jack and Peter were both soaked.

"Daddy said Rusty was smiling at us," Jack says every time.

"Well," I say, and I'm smiling too, "labradors do sometimes look as if they're smiling – their lip gets caught up at one side.

Jack nods. "He was smiling – Daddy and me knew," he says.

So yes, I have moved on. And I can bring out the old memories, like old photos, and I can treasure every single one.

Jack is nearly ten now, and so like Peter. The same brown eyes, the same fair hair. My chin, with a small dimple in it, and I'm afraid the same freckles on his nose. So yes, he is very much our son, mine and Peter's.

He comes in now, from taking Rusty for his walk, looking more than a little troubled.

"Rusty didn't want to go to the common," he tells me. "He just sat down, and looked at me, and he **Continued overleaf...**

Continued from previous page
walks so slow now, Mummy."

Lying on the kitchen floor, Rusty wags his tail apologetically. He is breathing really very heavily, and that bothers me.

"I think we'd better take him to see Rob," Jack says softly, and his voice isn't quite steady.

"Yes, I think we should," I say, and I remember what Rob, our vet, said quietly to me, after our last visit and my heart sinks.

"We bought him some extra time with that new medication, but – he is an old dog after all, and he's had a pretty good life."

I've told Jack some of this, but I'm not sure whether he really understands, although last Saturday, when Rob came with us to the beach for a picnic, Jack did talk about Rusty to him.

I give Rusty his supper, and he eats a little of it, then, still apologetic, he leaves the rest, and lies down again, giving little sounds of discomfort.

I look at the clock on the kitchen wall. Rob's surgery time is over, but with luck he will still be there.

"Rob?" I say into the receiver, and I don't have to tell him it's me. "Rob, can we bring Rusty to see you now?"

"Of course, Laura," Rob says, "right away," as I knew he would.

He's waiting for us when we park outside the surgery, and he lifts Rusty out of the car, very gently. Rusty knows him so well, and even now, he's glad to see him.

"Me and Mummy lifted him in together," Jack tells him. "He's quite heavy, Rob."

He sets our old dog down gently, slipping a blanket on the table first. We watch, Jack and I, silently, as Rob's strong brown hands, move over Rusty's whole body, pausing when we all hear Rusty's little intake of breath when something hurts. I wince myself.

I know what he has to tell us, before he says anything.

"Jack," he says, at last, "remember we said that as long as Rusty was enjoying his food, and his walks, then he would still have a good enough quality of life?"

Jack nods, not saying anything.

Rob hesitates for a moment. It's tough on him, telling Jack this, but I know it's better coming from him. He looks at me and I give him a small encouraging nod.

"Well, I think that has changed now, Jack," Rob says, and his hand on our old dog's head is gentle. So gentle that Rusty is almost asleep.

"Rusty is a tired old dog, and most of the time he doesn't feel very well," his voice is gentle.

Jack puts his small hand on Rusty's silky coat too, and the stump of a tail wags just a little bit.

"I know you're going to give him an injection, and let him go to sleep," Jack says now, and amazingly, his voice is almost steady, composed even.

"Could you do it right now, Rob, while you and me and Mummy are with him?" he asks.

Rob says that he can, and now I move closer to Rusty too, and there are tears blurring my eyes.

Pictures flash before my eyes: the small bundle of golden fur Peter brought for my birthday, three years before Jack was born; baby Jack crawling, and the dog

and carries him to his own station-wagon. He comes home with us, and we bury Rusty under his favourite tree in the garden.

We stand there, for a little while, and my eyes are still blurred with tears even when we leave.

Jack cries, too, that night, but somehow I can see that they are healing tears. And the next day, when I have moved Rusty's bed out to the garage, he stops me from taking his lead and his collar from

We were both still healing from one loss – another seemed far too soon

beside him, anxious, caring. Rusty always at our side during the long months when Peter was so ill; the way he used to look up hopefully at Jack and me, after Peter had died, looking beyond us, for the one who wasn't there any more.

"Oh, Rusty," I say, unsteadily. For a moment, Rob's hand covers mine, and I'm grateful for that.

"Everything is ready now," Rob says. "Just keep on holding his paw, Jack – he knows you're there, he knows we're all here with him."

And so Rusty goes to sleep, gently, peacefully, gracefully.

When we're sure he's gone, Jack kisses him, for the last time, and so do I. Everyone is silent.

"Thank you, Rob," I say, not quite steadily.

Rob wraps Rusty in the blanket,

the hook beside the door.

"I don't want Rusty's lead taken away," he says firmly. And then, surprising me, "I like seeing it there. I like remembering him."

As the days pass, there are times when both Jack and I have a little weep, at the strangeness of our house with Rusty not there. Rob looks in one morning, between surgery times, to see how we're doing. Jack, of course, is at school, but we sit at the kitchen table and drink coffee.

I tell him that Jack had asked me that morning if Rob would be able to come to watch him playing soccer on Saturday.

"Of course," Rob says. "As long as Jack understands I may have to **Continued overleaf…**

leave if there's an emergency call on my mobile."

"Yes, he understands," I answer.

For a moment, Rob looks at me steadily, a question in his eyes. A question I don't feel I can give him an answer to just yet.

After a moment, his hand covers mine, on the kitchen table, and it's really comforting.

Comforting and – safe, somehow. For a little while, I feel that I could go on forever, sitting like that, with Rob's hand on mine. But – but…

"It's all right, Laura," he says, quietly, gently. "Really."

He stands up, and says he'll see us on Saturday. I nod.

I don't know what it is that holds me up, that stops me from taking the next step. Sometimes, I think I'm afraid to let myself love again; afraid, perhaps, of loving and losing yet again.

I know this is so foolish, but I can't help it. And sometimes I think I feel guilty, that I could even let myself love again.

Peter would want me to love again, I know he would. He knew Rob, and he liked him, and he wouldn't want me to be alone.

Mostly, though, I just don't know why I hold back.

It's a cold afternoon on Saturday, and I'm huddled in my seat, watching Jack's school team playing, when Rob arrives and sits down beside me.

"Had to check on some new arrivals," he tells me. "Mary Robinson's Holly had her pups a few days ago. One of them was struggling a bit, but they're all fine now. And she's absolutely delighted they're all black."

Holly is a black Labrador, and was one of Rusty's doggy chums – we often met in the park.

We shout when Jack almost scores a goal, and then Rob turns to me.

"Mary Robinson was saying that she promised Jack he could come to see Holly's pups when they were born," he says carefully.

It's only a week since Rusty went, and I think right away that it would hurt Jack too much to see Rusty's friend, with her pups. Rob sees this in my eyes.

"We should ask him, Laura," he says, and I know he's right.

Jack's team doesn't win, but they played well, we tell Jack. His cheeks are rosy, his hair tousled, and he says – to Rob, not to me, because he knows soccer is more Rob's thing than mine, "It was a good game, wasn't it?" And Rob agrees enthusiastically.

I know Pete would want me to love again – I don't know why I'm holding back

We go to the tearoom round the corner. Rob and I have coffee, and Jack has hot chocolate. I'm wondering how to mention Holly's pups, when Jack looks across at me, a small moustache of chocolate foam on his rosy face.

"It feels longer than a week, doesn't it, Mummy?" he says, and I don't have to ask what he means.

And then, unexpectedly, he says, to both of us, "I was thinking, at first, that it isn't fair, that dogs have such a short life. I know Rusty was thirteen, and that makes him —" he pauses "— more than ninety, if he was a person, and that's awful old. But – but thirteen years isn't very long at all, is it?"

"No, Jack, it doesn't seem very long," Rob agrees.

"But I was thinking more, and you know what? People have to live for a long time, so that they can learn things, like – like living a good life, loving everyone, being nice to everyone."

He puts his empty mug down, and smiles at us. "And dogs know that right from the start, so they don't have to stay as long."

"I think that makes a lot of sense, Jack," I say, not quite steadily, thinking how wonderful this is, my thoughtful son working all this out, on his own.

Without being asked, Rob passes me his large white handkerchief, and I dry my eyes. And I know it's all right, when Rob tells Jack about Holly's pups.

"Could we go and see them, Rob?" Jack asks. "If you're coming for tea, we could go and see them on our way home."

Rob raises his eyebrows, and I nod. I want him with me, when Jack sees the puppies, in case the sight of the pups makes the loss of Rusty too much for him, in spite of his wonderful thoughts.

Jack runs ahead of us, up the path, and rings the bell.

"Can I see Holly's puppies, Mrs Robinson?" he asks, breathlessly, and she takes his hand and they go to the kitchen.

Holly is in her basket with five wriggling puppies close to her. She knows us well, but for a moment I have a pang, sure she will look for Rusty and upset Jack.

Jack kneels down. Gently, he touches a small velvet head.

"It's all right, Holly, I won't hurt your puppies," he says softly. He **Continued overleaf…**

Continued from previous page

looks up. "Do you think I could hold one of them, Mrs Robinson?"

Mary Robinson lifts one of the pups, and puts it in Jack's arms.

Gravely, he inspects the puppy from head to toe, tells us she's a girl, and then he just holds her, his cheek against the soft fur.

"She wants to go back to her

There will be other puppies. And – you loved Rusty so much."

My son shakes his head.

"It's all right, Mummy," he tells me and frowns. "I don't want this puppy to take Rusty's place, you know. No puppy could ever, ever do that. But it's because I loved Rusty so much, that I can really love this puppy, too.

If Jack is ready to take a chance on loving again, why can't I?

mother now," he says sensibly, and he puts her back beside Holly and the other pups.

We thank Mary for the viewing, and she tells Jack he can come to visit any time at all.

Jack is quiet for the rest of the way home, then, when the three of us are in the house, he says to Rob, "How old will Holly's puppies have to be when they can leave her?"

I hold my breath, knowing where this is all leading.

"Seven or eight weeks is best," Rob tells him, and his eyes meet mine, hopefully.

"Mummy," Jack says. "Could we have that puppy I was holding? When she's old enough to leave her mother, I mean?"

I take his small face between my hands and look into his eyes.

"Are you sure, Jack?" I ask him. "It's quite soon after Rusty dying – maybe you need a little longer.

"So can we have her?"

It isn't easy to speak, but after a moment I say yes, he can, and he goes off to phone Mary Robinson. He is only ten, my son, but in this moment of simplicity, he has made me see everything so very clearly.

"What are you thinking, Laura?" Rob asks me. And I know how much this matters to him – to us.

I take a deep breath.

"I'm thinking," I say, very steadily, "that my son Jack is a very wise little boy."

"So am I." Rob says. "So am I."

ABOUT THE AUTHOR

"I wrote this as we were about to say goodbye to our old collie," Isobel says. "The important things in my life are all my family, our dogs and reading and writing."

The Final Piece

You'll be hooked on this intriguing story of an obsessive husband and a wife whose patience has finally run out

By Jenny Robson

How cosy and comforting it is here in my workroom. It always has been, even at the worst times when Howard's constant criticisms drove me to despair.

My sunflower mosaic is coming along nicely, a work of art already. Just like the other completed mosaics that adorn the walls: my mountain scenes, my seascapes. Amazing what you can do with broken crockery!

That's where most of my tesserae come from: all the plates **Continued overleaf…**

Continued from previous page
and mugs and dishes I have smashed over the years. Smashing plates has always been my way of dealing with the stress of living with Howard – and since my current dinner service is yellow, what better choice of subject for my mosaic than sunflowers?

"Tesserae?" repeats Detective Inspector Daniel Evans. He sits there in my comfortable armchair, watching while I work.

I smile at him. "It's what we call the pieces we stick into the grout," I explain. "A single piece is called a tessera, I think. It's in Latin, or something. You can use anything for tesserae. Shells, glass, beads. I like using broken crockery."

I do not explain why I have so much broken crockery. But the Detective Inspector already knows the ins and outs of my unhappy marriage to Howard. From the start of the investigation, I haven't tried to hide anything.

"No, Detective Inspector, we aren't – weren't – happily married. Howard is – was – an extremely pernickety, petty man who lived by his watch."

Detective Inspector Evans – Daniel – reminds me of a Teddy bear, the kind of Teddy bear you just want to hug. He is big, softly-spoken and slow-moving. So different from bony, uptight Howard who was always checking his darned watch.

I pick up my hammer and tap sharply at a shard of yellow soup-bowl. I use just the right amount of force so that the awkward edges sheer off cleanly. I have become a master over the years. My tesserae are works of art in themselves.

"Actually, we need to talk about your late husband's watch," Daniel says and opens his notebook. But I feel no anxiety. I know this is all pretence. Just an excuse for him to spend the evening here with me and away from his endless reports and paper-laden desk.

I pick up the small yellow tessera with my tweezers and lay it carefully in place on the grout. My

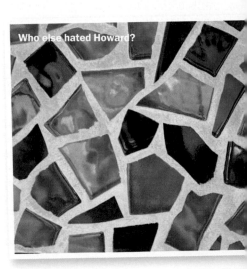

Who else hated Howard?

second sunflower is slowly filling out. This is what I love about mosaic work: the way what is useless and pointless can be transformed into something totally unique and beautiful.

It is what I intend doing with my life too. I will pick up the shattered pieces and turn them into something worthwhile. And Daniel? Will he become a tessera of my new life? I hope so. I long to

habits, that was my husband.

Or, "Margaret, why haven't you wheeled my golf-cart to the front door yet? It's after eight-ten."

Or worst of all. "Ten-fifteen, Margaret. I expect my conjugal rights by half-past. You have fifteen minutes to get ready."

Sometimes, I used to steal that damned watch of his – while he was in the shower, or in the early hours when I couldn't sleep for the

The pride I felt in my ability was great – the last piece fitted perfectly

walk over to the armchair and seat myself on his Teddy bear lap and wait for him to wrap his Teddy bear arms around me. Despite the notebook in his hand.

"What is it that you want to know about Howard's watch?" I ask quite pleasantly.

I wasn't married to a flesh-and-blood man. I was married to a wrist-watch with a robot attached to it. That watch ruled my life with its big numbered face behind the blue-tinted glass. With its industrial-strength hands moving forward, ever forward and always catching me out.

"Margaret, it's already six-o-seven. Why isn't supper ready? You know I prefer to eat immediately after my five-forty-five shower!" A man of absolute and regimentedly unchangeable

anger boiling up inside me. I would take his watch to my workroom and turn those industrial-strength hands backwards. Yes, backwards.

Just five, ten minutes backwards. It was a struggle. The winder was as stiff and un-giving as the watch's owner. But it's amazing what you can do when you're really determined. I became quite a master at shifting those accusing hands.

Then I would laugh silently as I looked through the blue-tinted glass at the time that was wrong, so wrong. The leather strap with its heavy buckle dangled helplessly.

Next day, Howard would be going berserk, late for meetings and appointments, threatening to take the watch back and demand a refund. He never suspected! Those **Continued overleaf...**

were days when I was in control and didn't feel any need to smash things up in the kitchen.

"What about Howard's watch?" I ask the Detective Inspector again.

Daniel still hasn't given me an answer. But that is what I love about him. He takes his time. Nothing is a rush or a panic. He is Teddy bear slow without any need to get uptight or bluster. He works on Teddy bear time.

And, of course, that is why he is here. Otherwise, he'd be back at the police station, following other leads in the case. Like trying to find out who else considered Howard a pain in the neck and wanted rid of him. Or like finding out who else knew that Howard would be alone that fateful Friday evening while I was bound for my sister's home in Merrifield some distance away.

I was the one who found Howard – three days later and he was not a pretty sight! I got back from my sister's on the Monday morning and there he was, face-down, his bony, naked body stretched out beside the shower – with the back of his head smashed in and one of his golf irons lying there on the bathroom floor. No fingerprints on it, of course. Wiped clean.

"Probably premeditated, in that case." So Detective Inspector Evans informed me that Monday afternoon. He also told me that I was a suspect – his Number One suspect. A wife is always the Number One suspect when a husband is found murdered, especially when there are neighbours who will testify to frequent arguments and plates smashing. "Also, there is no sign of forced entry," the Detective Inspector pointed out that Monday afternoon not long ago.

I sat hunched on the sofa, the grieving widow. Well, it is a shock to find your husband dead on the bathroom floor, naked apart from his beloved wrist-watch!

"That's because I forgot to lock the front door when I left," I answered, looking up into his gentle eyes. And even though I was suspect Number One, I was already appreciating the slow, laid-back charm of this policeman. Especially when he gently, sympathetically, stroked my hand.

"And exactly what time did you leave home?" Even while D. I. Evans questioned me, I felt safe and secure in his presence.

"Around six o'clock," I answered. "I caught the six-thirty train to Merrifield. My sister and

He had to question everybody – but I knew how he really felt about me

calling me Mrs Mullins at this point. "It seems pretty evident that you left home by eighteen-hundred on the Friday night. And since the murder was only committed at nineteen-fifty-three…"

He had a lovely face, Detective Inspector Evans. I was still calling him Detective Inspector Evans at this point. Only proper.

That was the other irony. It was Howard's blue-tinted watch that saved me, that took me off the suspect list. It was found smashed on his lifeless arm, the blue-tinted glass shattered on the bathroom tiles, the industrial-strength hands showing the exact moment of the crime: seven minutes to eight. And of course, at that precise moment, I was well on my way to Merrifield, looking forward to a peaceful weekend away from Howard and his endless petty demands.

Daniel leans back in my armchair now, looking relaxed despite the notebook in his hand. "You see, Maggie. There's a small problem with your husband's watch. And I just need to clear it up with you if that's all right."

My second sunflower is nearly complete now. Proud and hopeful **Continued overleaf…**

her husband met me at the station – at eight-twenty. You can check the railway timetable. You can check with my sister."

It was strange, ironic, how time had suddenly become my ally. After all the years of it being my hated enemy! Because, yes, these times gave me a watertight alibi. Everything checked out. The Detective Inspector came to tell me this the following day.

It seems that everything pans out, Mrs Mullins." He was still

Continued from previous page
and unafraid in the drying grout. But I need a few green leaves to balance the picture. I will have to buy a few green plates and smash them. Not in anger, of course. Just out of necessity.

But perhaps I can use some of the bathroom tiles? They are a lovely deep green. And a few of them are chipped now because of Howard's fall. I just need to wash off the last smears of blood...

"You see, Maggie, I collected all the pieces of glass still stuck to the wrist-watch at the scene of the crime. And I picked up the few pieces lying on the bathroom tiles beside the body. Then I tried to fit them all together. But they don't

with two-and-a-half spoonfuls per cup. No wonder he was always dashing about in a frenzy.

I put my little hammer down on the table. I peel off my surgical gloves. Surgical gloves are a must for a worker in mosaic. They keep your hands clean and free from the sticky grout. And I must admit, it is a peculiarly satisfying feeling, snapping them off your hands when you're finished.

I go off to the kitchen to heat the milk, humming happily. The house has a lovely atmosphere now that Howard is no longer dashing around it like some wound-up, neurotic robot. In the cupboard I see that I have only a couple of mugs left. The others were

He'd been skinny and wound-up, like his watch – but Daniel was a Teddy bear

make a full circle. There seems to be a piece missing."

I shrug and shake my head. I know dear Daniel is just playing his part well, pretending he is here on official business.

Perhaps policemen are like therapists and doctors? Perhaps there is some code of conduct that forbids them to have relationships with ex-suspects?

"How about a cup of Milo?" I offer. Daniel enjoys my Milo, the drink of the calm, easygoing man. Howard always drank pure coffee

smashed during the pre-murder days. Their pieces are already part of my mosaic collection – my seascapes – since they provided me with deep torquoise tesserae.

I take my time making the Milo. There is no rush. With Daniel, nothing is ever hurried. He will wait for me quietly in my workroom. And perhaps when he has had his Milo, perhaps then he will decide it is finally time.

Perhaps he will reach out to me at last and hold me against his

difficult but I take pleasure in doing things slowly and carefully.

And the errant piece of blue-tinted watch glass? Well, it is safely hidden now, one more tessera in my final seascape, the one with the seagulls swooping - a real work of art! In so many tones of blue.

Humming still, I carry the mugs of steaming, delicious Milo back to my workroom.

Teddy bear chest. The best things in life are always worth waiting for. Howard never understood that.

The missing piece of watch glass doesn't worry me either. It is safely hidden. I found it there on my work-table, luckily before the police did! Where else would it be?

After all, I had taken Howard's wrist-watch to my workroom whilst he had his five-forty-five shower that fateful Friday. And I'd wound the hands, forward this time, to seven minutes to eight. Then I'd brought my little hammer down on the watch-face with just the right amount of force. After which, I collected Howard's heaviest golf iron...

There was the slight problem of buckling the wrist-watch back on to Howard's lifeless arm. The surgical gloves made it quite

But Daniel seems to have lost his Teddy bear charm altogether. He is standing now, stepping like a bloodhound towards the far wall.

"Perhaps I should take a look at these seascapes of yours," he says. "Just to satisfy myself that you haven't used any blue-tinted glass tesserae in any of them!"

That is when I drop the mugs - my last two mugs. They lie in shattered turquoise shards on the floor in my workshop.

ABOUT THE AUTHOR

Rising between 4.30 and 5am, Jenny begins her writing, knowing that almost everyone else is still in bed fast asleep

Fancy That!

Fascinating facts that make you go "wow"!

Heavy Eaters

The average Italian eats 33 kilos of pasta over the course of a year

WOW! ● **Dido is the most successful female singer Britain has ever produced. Her first two albums have sold more than 22 million copies.**

● Despite having a population of 7.36 million, 30% of London is open space, including more than 150 parks and public gardens.

Fact!

Licence To Kill, starring Timothy Dalton and Carey Lowell was the 16th James Bond spy film

● **Queueing is the only common word with five vowels in a row.**

Time For A Story

Since Noddy's creation 60 years ago, his 24 books by Enid Blyton have sold more than 200 million copies in 27 languages

WOW! ● It is technically incorrect to refer to a book's "ISBN number", as the "N" actually stands for "number". The other letters stand for International Standard Book.

● **The word petition comes from the Latin peto, meaning "I ask."**

● There are two teaspoonfuls in a dessertspoon and two dessertspoonfuls in a tablespoon.

Indian Idealist

Mahatma Gandhi married when he was 13 and worked as a barrister in London before becoming a political activist

● During the 1950s, airport vending machines sold life insurance policies in case of crashes.

● 58% of British women own more than 10 pairs of shoes, with 10% admitting to a stash of more than 31 pairs.

WOW! ● The term A1, to describe something good, originated in Edward Lloyd's Register of Ships, first printed in 1765, which used a combination of letters and numbers to grade the condition of vessels. A1 was considered the best.

WOW! ● Pat Boone and Roy Orbison both studied geology at the North Texas State University.

In The Swim

On average, 70 people try to swim the Channel each year. Less than half succeed

● **Chewing parsley can cure bad breath.**
● Eddie Izzard is 5' 7" tall.

Not Amused

For her Golden Jubilee, Queen Victoria was given a novelty bustle that played God Save The Queen when she sat down

Fact!

The legendary Hollywood actor, Humphrey Bogart's middle name was DeForest

The Lychee Tree

Enjoy this tale of a village guild saved by the appearance of a familiar stranger

By Amanda Thomas

L aura looked around the disappointing turn out, again. If this kept up, the village guild would not survive another year.

"Good evening, Jean, no Linda tonight?" Laura said.

"No, she hurt her back gardening at the weekend. Oh, Betty and Isabel can't make it either, something about tennis elbow."

"What, both of them?"

Jean shrugged. "Apparently."

Laura frowned as a couple of the other ladies added apologies from four more guild members.

"Well, I've said it before and I'll have to say it again, ladies, if we can't do better than this, we will have to disband, we won't be able to afford to rent the hall."

"Couldn't we have it in each other's houses? I think part of the problem is that some of the ladies don't want to come all the way out here of an evening," Jean said.

"All the way out here? We're only two minutes out of the village! Honestly, anyone would think we were a bunch of octogenarians, no offence Mabel."

"None taken, dear." Mabel looked up from her knitting briefly.

"Well, there's a case in point, Mabel *is* a paid up octogenarian and she doesn't find the journey here too arduous."

Laura looked down at her papers.

"It's a great pity really, the summer is on its way and we're being invited to compete in various events against other villages. But at this rate I don't think we would even be able to raise enough ladies for a team. Take this one for example, a knit-off, against Upper Pilling." Mabel paused mid purl and Laura smiled at her.

"Well, obviously Mabel would be our star turn but the team needs to be made up of eight knitters. There are only six of us here tonight and I for one can't knit!"

"Nor can I," said Jean.

Laura sighed. "And then there is the team for the annual church

Between the lush leaves, tiny fruits were growing

flower arrangement contest at Middle Pilling. That would need at least five of us but the standard is pretty high and even with a full complement, we would be hard pressed to select enough of us to stand a chance of winning."

"I'd like to do that one," Jean said. Laura held her hands up. "So would I, Jean but without a proper turn out of members…"

Continued overleaf…

"Anything else?" one of the other ladies asked surreptitiously, looking at her watch.

"One other thing but I'm not even going to consider it. I can put the other two on hold for a week before I reply so that you ladies can try and coax other members to come back to the fold."

"Well, what is it?" Jean asked.

"What is what?"

"The other thing, the one you are not even going to consider?"

"Oh, that, it's a tug-of-war between the five Pillings.

"Apparently, following the keep fit drives that have been going on in the villages through the winter, it was thought this might be a good way of celebrating the new level of fitness of Pilling ladies. But with bad backs and tennis elbows and – what was it Susan had, Madge? Oh, yes, clicky knees – I don't think we would really be in the running for that, do you?"

"Pity," Jean said. "It sounds like it could have been fun."

The next morning, as Laura left the bakery in Lesser Pilling, the twins, Isabel and Betty approached her. Laura liked the spinster twins whom she'd known since childhood.

"We heard about the tug-of-war, Laura, when is it?"

Laura was taken aback. "Where did you hear about that?"

"Jean," they said together. "And at church on Sunday one of our cousins from Greater Pilling told us that a very nice man who used to live here was going to coach their team. He's going to come to train each team one day a week," Betty said looking at her sister and winking slyly.

"Well, you'll just have to come along to the next meeting, you and all the others. We could hardly pull a curtain with the turn-outs we've been getting lately, let alone a tug-of-war rope! Sorry to rush ladies but I've got a dentist's appointment. Bye!" Laura called as she mounted her bicycle, waved goodbye over her shoulder and promptly forgot all about the tug-of-war.

As Laura leaned her bike against the wall of the village hall on the evening of the next meeting, she was surprised to see quite a few more cars than usual in the car park.

Inside the hall she was momentarily stopped in her tracks as a sea of faces turned towards her. There must be at least 20 ladies there, some of whom Laura had not seen for months.

After welcoming the members, Laura began to go through the calendar for the coming months. She could sense restlessness in the room and although hands went up for the knit-off and the flower arranging, she couldn't help feeling she was being hurried along.

Eventually, unable to contain themselves, Betty and Isabel said in unison: "So what about the tug-of-war?" There was an audible

earlier encounter with the twins in Lesser Pilling.

Laura found the tug-of-war announcement stuck with a coffee cup stain to one about a collection of old clothes for Central America. Living as they did on a windswept side of Dartmoor, Laura was not too sure how Ugg boots and chunky knits would go down in the rain forest, but that was beside the point at the moment. She read out the short list of instructions on the tug-of-war leaflet to the group.

"Each team should be made up of ten 'tuggers' with three in reserve." She looked around the room; the ladies were on the edge of their seats. Laura was stunned by the response, but if this is what it took to keep the guild alive, well, she was all in favour.

"Anyone would think we were a bunch of octogenarians, no offence Mabel."

murmur along the rows of seats and Laura looked around the room in amazement. Surely this was not what they'd all turned out for? An inter village tug-of-war?

Laura was not even sure that she'd brought the announcement and entry form with her, so certain had she been that they wouldn't be entering a team. She had completely forgotten her

"The first practice will be on Wednesday at 3pm outside on the playing field. I'll put the list here for you to sign up if you're interested."

On Tuesday evening, Laura sat in the late spring sunshine at the back of her cottage looking through the information that had arrived that morning for the tug-of-
Continued overleaf...

Continued from previous page
war. She was looking for the name of the coach who would be joining their session the next afternoon.

When she found it, she stared at it in shock for a moment before her fingers loosened and the paper fluttered on to the lawn. Scrabbling

over to where the plant, now five foot tall, was having an outing on the patio for the day. It was still too cool for it to be left out in the garden all night, and Laura would take it in to its spot next to the French windows before nightfall.

She had tended the plant over

With the seed was a card: "If you can wait, I'll be back to share the fruit"

around after it, Laura read the name again. Josh Penn. She felt heat suffuse her face.

As she sat back on her chair, she could see his face as it had been all those years ago, before he left the village, begging her to come with him to explore the world. But she had been quite unable to think of defying her parents with such a scandalous plan and really, if she were honest, she was a home bird, quite comfortable in her little corner of England.

From time to time she had heard of Josh and his escapades in far-flung places from his parents with whom she'd remained close.

Five years after he left, on her 30th birthday, a seed, beautifully wrapped in a small woven box, had arrived from China, with instructions on how to plant and care for it and a beautiful card – *If you can wait, I'll be back to share the fruit with you.*

It was a lychee tree. Laura looked

the years and every year it displayed beautiful leaves but never any fruit. Still, Laura loved the plant. After Josh's parents had died, his sister, Milly, had moved to Spain and Laura had heard nothing more of her first and only love.

Her mouth was dry and, all of a sudden, she remembered her encounter with Betty and Isabel. They'd mentioned that a man was coming to coach, seemed quite excited at the prospect, she recalled. Did they know already that it was Josh?

She closed her eyes. They had all been at school together and in fact everyone had assumed that she and Josh would get married. And they might have done if he had not had wanderlust or she'd had a bit more courage.

Arriving at the village hall the next afternoon, Laura felt the butterflies in her stomach threaten to rob her of her voice. She hoped that her tennis shorts and jumper would be appropriate; she was not entirely sure what the dress code for tug-of-war was.

As she looked around at the ladies who'd turned out, she could see she was not alone in her uncertainty of what to wear. A couple of track suits rustled in the chairs to her right, a few golfing trousers nestled together near the back and, to her right, a mish mash of tennis, netball and plain leisure shorts and trousers made up the rest of the hall.

She wondered how on earth they were going to make the selection as it seemed that almost every member of the guild was dressed to try out for the team.

Still, that would not be her problem, it was Josh's. As the thought formed in her mind she felt her face flush. She could not believe that she would soon be seeing him again after all these years.

To add to her butterflies, her legs seemed to have gone weak now, and she waited for all the ladies to leave the hall before she ventured out on to the playing fields in the warm sunshine.

The ladies had gathered in the centre of the field and Laura could see on each side of the crowd, peeping out of the grass, either end of a rope. As she drew closer, like the parting of the Red Sea, they moved away leaving a lone figure standing in front of her.

"Laura!" Josh said. "What a lovely surprise!"

Laura felt twenty pairs of eyes swivel towards her.

"Hello, Josh." Laura's voice came out as a squeak.

The eyes swivelled back to Josh, like avid spectators at a tennis match. For a moment Josh looked perplexed and then glancing at Laura, her face flushed, he suddenly clapped his hands.

"Right ladies, let's be having you!" And before long, he had them lined up on either side of the rope, going through the rules with them and, as tactfully as possible, trying to position the more robust ladies in the optimum positions.
Continued overleaf...

Continued from previous page

As Laura sorted out the printed leaflets with the rules on them for the ladies, Josh asked if she would be taking part.

"No, thanks, I think we have enough ladies, don't you?"

"Nonsense, come on, there's a slot for you here." And Laura fell in without protest.

"Right, I'm going to demonstrate with Laura." Josh moved up behind her and put his hands over hers, moving them along the rope until they were the right distance apart, moving her fingers so that her grip on the rope was correct.

Out of the corner of her eye Laura could see the twins, their eyes wide, watching her and Josh, and she knew it was not just the intricacies of correct technique that was enthralling them.

As she looked down at her hands, she was very aware of the strong, smooth brown arms and powerful hands against her own. The smell of Josh, with just the hint of subtle aftershave, took her ladies opposite, she studied him.

He was unmistakably Josh, although his hair was now a steely grey, his face told the tale of a life spent outdoors. Deep laughter lines were etched around his eyes and a light stubble grazed his strong jaw. He was still slim and muscular – and very attractive.

Despite herself, Laura could not stop her eyes wandering to his ring finger. It was bare.

By the end of the session, Laura could see she was not the only one looking speculatively at Josh.

He was an excellent and inspirational teacher and there wasn't a single drop-out.

"Well, ladies, I'm going to have to be tougher on you next time. We need to get our team identified. I can't say, of course, how the other Pillings are doing but suffice to say we need to get a wriggle on."

Laura smiled, as Josh used a phrase she had heard him use many times before. As the ladies left, she shuffled and sorted the papers on her desk in the hall a

She could picture his face, begging her to come with him to explore the world

reeling back 25 years, and she realised that the cologne he had on was the same one he'd worn all those years ago. *Was it Chanel*, she wondered. As he moved away from her and started to instruct the dozen times until finally he appeared at the door.

"Laura? I'm off now, see you next week, same time?" And with that he was gone.

Gathering her papers, she made

for her car. She felt stupid – like a silly schoolgirl. What had she expected? A date? Whatever relationship they'd had was now 25 years in the past. But she'd thought they might have exchanged a few words. It was almost as though he'd forgotten they'd once been "an item" as they said these days.

At home, Laura was just putting her lychee tree back inside for the night when her doorbell went. Glancing at her reflection in the hall mirror, Laura opened the door.

It was her friend, Jean.

"Oh, hello, Jean." Laura couldn't resist looking up the road.

"Hello, Laura, are you expecting someone?" Jean smiled mischievously.

"Of course not, come in." Laura made Jean a cup of tea as her friend talked excitedly about the tug-of-war team.

"I do hope I get picked. It's such fun, don't you think so?" Laura didn't think so. This was not how she had imagined her first meeting with Josh after all these years.

She had imagined that they would talk over old times, catch up with each other's lives. And now she felt as though she really didn't want to see him again, it was too awkward, and she really didn't know how to be around him, especially under the watchful eyes of the rest of the village guild.

In fact, she realised, she felt angry with him for throwing her into this turmoil. She was quite happy with her life, did not want these feelings raked up from the past.

"I *said*, Laura, I thought Josh was looking extremely well. It's not fair how men age so much better than we do."

"Sorry?"

"Oh, come on Laura, spill the beans, we haven't forgotten, you know – any of us!"

"Haven't forgotten what?"

"That you and Josh used to see each other, before he went away."

Well, I think he has, Laura thought to herself. Out loud she said, "Oh, Jean, that was a lifetime ago, ancient history, I had hardly given it a thought."

"Hmm," Jean said, obviously
Continued overleaf...

unconvinced. "Strange though, that neither of you married."

"What?" Laura almost spilled her cup of tea.

"Oh, yes, Isabel asked him outright! You know Isabel!"

"And Josh said that he had never…?"

"No, never married," Jean interrupted triumphantly.

That night, her mind was so active, Laura hardly slept a wink.

Whardly came up, she went wearily downstairs and put the kettle on. She opened the French windows and put the lychee tree outside.

A heavy bundle of manuals arrived in the post for her to translate. Normally she enjoyed losing herself in the Russian that she had learned from her mother. It was a career that had served her well over the years and her natural aptitude for languages had led her eventually to add French and Italian to her repertoire.

But it was Russian she loved, the richness of the language, the memory of her mother's voice telling her stories of her own childhood in Moscow; her family, now all gone, and a life that Laura could only imagine, a million miles away from her childhood in the wild landscape of Dartmoor.

But today it was a chore and her mind kept wandering. Obviously

Josh had no interest in a stroll down memory lane with her and she had better stop seeing him as an old flame and start seeing him as… what? It was all too maddening.

On the playing field again a week later, Josh called hello to her, and several of the others including Jean, Betty and Isabel. This time he did not single her out to demonstrate on and when the final cut for the team was announced, she had not made it.

"Sorry, Laura, you're a bit too tall, you're raising the rope, and we need ladies of equal height."

Laura stood back and watched for a while before going back into the hall. This time Josh did not even pop his head around the door and she eventually emerged from the hall to an empty car park.

In the week before the next tug-of-war coaching session, Laura bumped into Josh twice, once at the pub where she was meeting Jean for lunch. He was standing at the bar with a couple of Upper Pilling men and, apart from a polite nod to Jean and Laura, he kept his back to them. The second meeting was in the queue at the post office. He came in behind her and greeted her warmly as they waited. But then he greeted everyone else just as warmly and apart from small talk, he gave no indication that he and Laura had been anything other than former school friends.

As the tug-of-war competition approached, the coaching sessions were stepped up to three times a week and Josh was kept busy coaching up to three teams an afternoon. At first Laura went to watch them but she felt like a spare part, like some sort of pushy mother hovering over her child, so she stopped going.

When finally the day of the competition came, Laura and Jean stood together behind their team as the knock-out competition wore on.

"Not a clicky knee or tennis elbow to be seen now!" Laura said to Jean as they cheered the ladies of the guild guild on.

"They do look nice in those matching shorts and T-shirts," Jean said. "And they're in the semi-finals! Well done, girls, well done!"

Josh was umpiring the match and Laura thought again how, from a distance, he looked hardly any older than when she'd waved him off all those years ago.

And then suddenly the contest was over, and they'd won!

Almost all the guild had turned out to watch or compete and Mabel, as their oldest member, received the cup on their behalf. The match had caught the imagination of the villages as a whole and Laura received more than a dozen enquiries from ladies wanting to join the guild.

Tired and relaxed after her day in the sun, Laura let herself into her cottage just as the sun was setting in all its glorious hues.

She poured herself a glass of wine and stood outside beside the lychee tree. As she watched the sun sinking into a crimson sky, she thought back 25 years. Had she over-exaggerated what there had been between them? Had the years **Continued overleaf...**

Had the years built up their romance in her mind to something it was not?

built up their romance in her mind to something it was not?

As she looked out over the garden, she thought of the night that Josh had told her sitting right here on the step outside, the one that she always put the lychee tree on, that he was leaving. They had both cried, he had held her in his arms, stroked her hair, and kissed her in the way that made her legs weak. She knew with every fibre of her body that they were meant for each other; that everything between them was in complete harmony. How could he go and leave half of himself behind?

No, she had not imagined it, in the half dark the feelings she had kept suppressed for many years flooded back. As though it were yesterday, she felt the pain of losing him, then the certainty that he would get half way around the world and then, missing her

"Josh," she whispered.

"I'm so sorry, Laura." In the moonlight, Laura thought she saw tears in his eyes. "I've been a coward, a miserable coward."

Laura could not speak.

"I've wanted to come to you so much, since I got back…" His voice faltered.

"Why didn't you?" Laura said.

Josh sat down on the step, as he had done all those years ago, drawing her down beside him.

"I felt so guilty. I never imagined that you'd be single when I got back, I should never have left but I did and now I feel that I may have robbed you of your chance for happiness… children."

Laura was speechless. Eventually she said, "You never married either?"

"No, I won't lie, I did come close a couple of times but the girls never matched up – to you," he said softly.

"There was me to come back for!" Laura cried brokenly, half angry, half sad

unbearably, come back to her. And then the months and years with hope fading, and finally dying. No, she had not imagined it.

A movement at the end of the garden caught her eye and suddenly Josh was beside her on the little cottage patio.

"Hello, Laura," he said gently.

"Then why didn't you come back?" Laura heard the anger in her voice, anger for the wasted years, what could have been.

Josh shrugged helplessly.

"I don't know, I had made a life for myself, I was sure you would have moved on. I visited Milly in Spain a couple of times, but you

even in the summer!"

As she leaned over to grasp the pot containing the lychee tree, her face brushed the leaves and she stopped. What was that? She put the plant down again and parted the leaves. It was fruit! Laura couldn't believe her eyes. She sat back on her heels, stunned.

"Look, Josh!" She pointed between the lush leaves where tiny fruits were growing. "It's never fruited before!"

They looked at each other.

"Do you remember what I wrote on the card?" Josh said taking her hands in his.

Laura nodded and he gently took her face in his hands and kissed her long and sweet.

"When the fruit are ripe, will we eat them together?" he asked, looking deep into her eyes.

As the years fell away and the sun finally slipped below the horizon, Laura looked up at him and smiled happily, gently smoothing the leaves of the lychee tree between her fingers.

"We've been waiting for you!"

and she had lost touch, and once my parents died, it seemed there was nothing to come back for."

"There was *me* to come back for!" Laura cried.

"I know, I know, I'm so sorry my beautiful, wonderful girl." He put his arms around her and drew her to him, holding her head on his shoulder and stroking her hair as her body shook with sobs.

When her sobbing subsided, he wiped the tears from her cheeks and his own.

"I see the lychee tree got to you," Josh said and Laura smiled through misted eyes. She felt a sense of relief as though her tears had washed away all the pain and tension of the long, lonely years without him.

"I take it in at night. I never trust the weather to be kind enough,

ABOUT THE AUTHOR

Amanda, who lives near Newbury, finds her best ideas come to her while out walking her spaniel, Paddy

Wishful Thinking

You'll smile as this sparkling story brings a sprinkling of fairy dust to Jane's somewhat unsatisfactory life. Read on and enjoy…

By Brenda Roberts

R eturning home to find a complete stranger fast asleep on your sofa is, it has to be said, not a thing that happens every day of the week. I found it very scary.

"Excuse me!" I boomed. The stranger, a woman dressed in a pink tutu, gently snored on. I gave her a wary tap on the shoulder, then stood well back.

She blinked and sat up, looking bewildered. "Wha–?"

I could see she was no thug, and I softened my tone. "Look, I'm not going to hurt you," I said. "But who are you and what on earth are you doing in my house?"

She went as pink as her dress. "Oh dear, this is frightfully embarrassing."

I began to lose patience. "Tell me who you are or I'll call the police."

"Goodness, dear, no need for that. Of course I must explain. Now, yes. I was returning from The United Fairy Conference, you see, when I came over rather fatigued. It had been a dreadfully long flight and I have rather weak wings, which runs in the family, I'm afraid; my grandmother suffered with them.

"Where were we? Ah yes, well, remembering all the advice about 'take a break', 'tiredness kills' and all that, I decided that popping in here for a nap would be the sensible thing to do."

I didn't understand a thing this woman was talking about. A long flight? A United Fairy Conference? Aching wings? Another thought

"You can call me Twinky"

"Ah, fairies have no need of keys, my love. Let me introduce myself. Twinky Sweetness. You may call me Twinky."

At that moment I got the wrong end of the stick. I thought I had been set up by some joker, and it was bad timing because I was in no mood for it. I had broken a tooth, leaving a sharp edge which had caused an ulcer on my tongue. It doesn't sound much, but it was so sore it made my head ache. Added to that I had received a statement from my bank that morning and a letter ticking me off for exceeding my overdraft. But worse than all of that, my heart had been broken by Mr Williams.

Mr Williams was the manager of the supermarket where I worked, and the object of all my desires. He was kind and considerate towards me, but totally unaware of the burning passion I felt for him. I couldn't bring myself to make the first move – I was far too timid. Then yesterday I saw him sharing an intimate joke with Gina Carter. Gina was a pretty **Continued overleaf…**

struck me suddenly. "How did you get in?" I demanded.

"The front door, actually."

None of this added up. Here was this person in fancy dress who, in my absence, had somehow entered my home and was now acting the innocent. "All my doors and windows are locked and you have no key," I said accusingly.

rosy-cheeked flirt, who worked on the delicatessen counter. Seeing them laughing together was like a stab in the heart.

"How did you enter my house?" I repeated sternly.

The woman smiled and touched my arm. "Come into the hallway, dear, and I will show you." Then, before my very eyes, she completely disappeared through the closed front door. Through the glass panel, I saw her shivering outside on the front step. She then melted back through the door to stand beside me again. Well, if this person really was a fairy, and it looked very much as though she was, I needed to sit down and try to get my head around it.

I retreated into the lounge and lowered myself into an armchair. "OK, I'm convinced," I said shakily. "Do fairies drink tea? I most

curls, held a jewelled butterfly at a jaunty angle. Her dress was typically fairy, tight fitting satin bodice and frothy, full skirt made from multitudinous layers of pink tulle. A sparkly stick with a star on the end, which I assumed was her magic wand, lay on her lap.

Fortified by the hot drink, I offered to make us something to eat. At once the fairy's eyes lit up. "Do you have primroses, dear?"

"I do have primroses in the garden but wouldn't you prefer a slice of ham in a nice crusty roll?"

Twinky tittered at this. "Fairies cannot eat foods like that, bless your heart, but a few delicate primrose flowers would be absolutely marvellous."

After her snack Twinky daintily patted her mouth with the napkin. "Now, my dear, I really must repay you for your kindness."

Before I could protest she waved

Aching wings? Fairy conference? Come on – who *was* this woman in pink?

certainly need a cup after that."

Her face broke into a grateful smile. "Oh my dear, how very kind, do you have camomile?"

I discreetly studied Twinky Sweetness while we drank. I had always imagined fairies to look like children but she didn't look particularly young. Her skin was clear and her hair, a mop of pink

her wand imperiously and spoke in a shrill voice. "I hereby grant you, Jane Baxter, three wishes."

Three wishes! One wish, if it worked, would be useful, but three! I thought of my broken tooth, my overdraft at the bank and, most of all, Mr Williams. I could turn these things around. I'd read stories of people being granted wishes,

invariably wasted by wishing silly things by mistake. I needed to be careful; I'd never get another chance like this.

"My first thought is to have my tooth fixed but that might be a waste of a wish," I told Twinky.

"I agree, sweetheart, why not just visit the dentist and save your wishes for something exciting?"

"I should have done something about my tooth today, but I always put off going to the dentist. I wish I wasn't such a wimp!"

I could have kicked myself. There! I'd wasted a wish already. Or perhaps I hadn't – I sensed a pleasant, warm confidence growing deep inside me. Suddenly, a feeling of such bravado swept through me that I determined to phone the dentist there and then.

"Well, done, dear," Twinky said encouragingly when I'd made my appointment there and then.

I thought it would be prudent to use my remaining two wishes before I wasted those, too. So I prepared to make these too without further ado.

"I, Jane Baxter, hereby wish for… lots of money!"

I had hoped that a pile of bank notes might appear before my eyes, but it didn't happen. Perhaps such a selfish, materialistic wish wouldn't quality. There might be conditions to this wishes lark. I began to feel uneasy and more than a little disappointed.

Nevertheless, I decided to make my third and dearest wish. "I, Jane Baxter, most humbly wish, with deep respect, that Mr Williams, manager of Carters Supermarket, would fall completely and hopelessly in love with me."

I was careful to keep my voice soft in case it made a difference. I didn't know quite how these things worked and for all I knew, there may have been some Chief Fairy who vetted these requests, allowing only those deemed to be fully deserving.

I'd entertained the wild hope that Mr Williams would appear in a flash, with eyes for no one but me. No such luck.

"Nothing has happened; will my last two wishes be granted, do you **Continued overleaf…**

Continued from previous page

think?" I asked anxiously.

Twinky tittered. "Try and be patient, my love."

Even if the money or Mr Williams' love did not materialise, at least I was no longer a pathetic wimp. I hadn't realised how good it felt to be brave, and there was no stopping me now. "I'm going to phone Mr Williams right away to ask if I could be considered for a supervisor's job; I need the extra money," I told Twinky. I didn't say I longed to hear his voice.

Twinky clapped her hands. "Bravo, Jane! Seize the moment!"

When I dialled the supermarket's number and asked to be put through to Mr Williams' office I was surprised by my own steady and confident voice.

"Hello, is that Mr Williams?" I asked chirpily. "This is Jane, Jane Baxter speaking."

"Oh, hello there, Jane, is everything all right?"

"Everything's fine, Mr Williams. I'm just calling to ask whether you would please bear me in mind when the next supervisor's job becomes vacant."

I could sense his surprise. I thought he sounded sort of impressed. "Well, Jane, if that's the case, then you've called at just the right time. Alison Wentworth, supervisor of Bakery, is expecting a happy event and has given in her notice this morning. Actually, I

think you might do very well in that position."

"Wonderful! Though of course, I'd expect a commensurate increase in my salary."

Another moment of silence. Then, sounding even more impressed, he told me that of course there would be a substantial salary increase. "Perhaps you would care to join me for dinner tonight? We could discuss the details in a more private setting."

My knees nearly went at that, but I remembered my new fearless status and I took a deep breath. "That would be great. Could you possibly pick me up?"

"Certainly, Jane. Half past seven? I know a nice little Moroccan restaurant quite near the Moreham by-pass."

When I put the phone down, Twinky clapped her hands again. "Splendid! Well done!"

Just then there was a tinkly little tune that seemed to come from the fairy's wand. "Excuse me, dear, I have a message." She flipped open

"Never mind," soothed Twinky. "At least you still have your three wishes, so you can wish for anything you like."

But there was nothing left that I wanted. As supervisor, I'd soon earn the extra money to pay off my overdraft and Mr Williams was

A wish is a powerful thing indeed – but sometimes other forces are at work too

a little hinged cover to the star on her wand and frowned.

"Well, would you believe it?" Twinky sighed. "I don't now how to tell you this but it's a message from headquarters – *regrettably your three wishes have failed as the service is temporarily unavailable. Please try again later.*"

Twinky clicked her teeth. "I've always said it was a mistake to computerise operations."

"But what does all this actually mean, Twinky?"

"It means, I'm afraid, that your wishes have not been processed and that you'll need to wish them all over again."

"But my newfound courage, my first wish – it was granted, I'm absolutely sure of it."

Twinky smiled. "That courage wasn't from my fairy magic, Jane. It all came entirely from you."

I was astonished. I could hardly believe I'd taken such initiative with no outside help.

taking me out to dinner. I rather wanted to pursue the rest of my desires by my own efforts.

So I shook my head. "I have everything I want, thank you. I'd like to donate my wishes to a worthy cause, if I can do that – I'll leave it up to you to choose."

Well, all that was a couple of years ago – and the new Mrs Williams owes her present state of happiness to Twinky and the wishes that didn't happen.

So if you should find a strange lady asleep on your sofa wearing a pink tutu, do be careful how you wake her won't you?

ABOUT THE AUTHOR

"Ideas pop into my head but disappear quickly, so I carry a pen and pad with me."

A Girl's Best Friend

A sparkling diamond ring, a devoted lover – how many of us have shared the same happy dream?

By Julie Dickins

How I've always wanted a real diamond! Since I was old enough to realise that the sort of ring you found at the bottom of a party bag covered in cake crumbs was not the real thing, I've yearned for a genuine "rock" from an exclusive jewellers. It wouldn't have to be huge, just big enough to twinkle in the sun and radiate a thousand sparkling lights across the room.

Of course, that's not all I longed for; in my often-rehearsed daydream the diamond would be accompanied by a millionaire lover in a designer suit. Undying love would shine from his dark eyes as he proposed on one knee in the plush surroundings of a five star hotel. Perfect! Just perfect!

Funnily enough, my dream didn't ever feature the jewellery counter at the supermarket, or a suitor in a dirty tracksuit with paint-splattered hands and an unshaven chin. Yet here we stood, my love and I, choosing an engagement ring. Just about as far from my dream as I could get!

"What about this one?" I said, holding up a solitaire attached to a square of black card.

"Looks like a proper diamond, does that!" Wayne slipped his arm around my shoulder and gave me a hug. "What d'ya say, love. D'ya want it, just as a temporary measure, of course?"

I held up the card with the ring attached. It looked like a diamond if you held it at arm's length and squinted. I could always pretend I'd bought it from the sort of exclusive jewellers where the staff call you "madam", invite you to be seated and pull out velvet-covered trays of glittery rings for "your perusal at your leisure".

I glanced across at my beloved

Every girl dreams of romance

who was trying to free the wheel of the supermarket trolley from a display stand full of special offer doughnuts and tried to imagine him in a designer suit. The nearest I could get was his "night out" gear; the same jeans and jacket combination which had punctuated the special events of our life together, from our first proper date to meeting my parents. He must have sensed my gaze and he turned and smiled back at me, fading my daydream with the warm reality of his love.

Continued overleaf…

Continued from previous page

I pushed the ring on to my finger with the card still attached.

Wayne took my hand. "It looks great, love, really chunky. Sparkly. Everyone'll notice it. Have a think. I'm off to check out the car mags. I'll meet you by the tills."

Wayne wandered off, taking the trolley full of groceries with him. I didn't blame him. He deserved a he'd proposed and I'd accepted.

We'd discussed wedding dates as we continued to fill the trolley and I was now about to choose my engagement ring from a rack near the checkouts. Oh, how dreams differ from reality!

I stretched out my fingers admiring my "rock". It felt right. It had a reassuring chunkiness, a weight that matched its life-

One minute we were buying fish, the next I was swept off my feet

bit of man-time with a motoring magazine. He'd done his fair share of emotional, girlie stuff today.

It had all started in the fish aisle as I cringed at the sight of the mackerel he'd chosen for tea.

"I'll never in a million years be able to chop their heads off," I'd told him honestly.

"Well, it's a good job you'll always have me to do it for you then, isn't it?" he'd said.

"Always?" I'd laughed.

"Yeah, always and forever, until the end of time, you know."

He'd smiled down at me and I'd looked back at him in the middle of the fish aisle and it was as if the lights went dim and a distant orchestra struck up.

"You know I love you, Angie. I always want to be with you. We could even get married, if you like."

Just like that, out of the blue, changing role. It glittered like a shining symbol of Wayne's love for me and the promise that we would always be together through good and bad times, husband and wife.

Husband and wife! The words sounded quaint and old-fashioned. Nan would approve. Marriage was the pinnacle of a woman's life according to Nan. She was thrilled when I decided to train to be a nurse, like her, eight years ago.

"Angie," she said, "you'll find good husband material at those parties nurses get invited to by all those junior doctors."

I had duly started my nurse's training and waited. There were plenty of parties but either the junior doctors were too

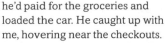

tired with all those long hours, or the hospital was deliberately recruiting party-shy men because there were never enough single attractive men to go round.

After a couple of years all the eligible doctors, fit and gorgeous physiotherapists and even the geekiest lab technicians had been snapped up. My tall, dark and handsome Mr Right turned out to be hospital maintenance man, Wayne, who swept me off my feet when he came to mend a leaky radiator on my ward.

So, two years later, here I was with the love of my life, choosing an engagement ring on a wintry Saturday afternoon at the supermarket. Only Wayne had wandered off somewhere!

When I eventually found him,

he'd paid for the groceries and loaded the car. He caught up with me, hovering near the checkouts.

"Over here, love," he yelled. "Let's get this thing paid for." He took the ring from me, looped his arm around my shoulder and squeezed. "You'll get a real diamond one day, love. I promise."

He kissed my cheek and, as I looked into his dark, smiling eyes, part of my dream was rekindled. His love shone out and my heart leapt to meet it.

On the way home, he talked about decorating the bathroom, how he'd seen some tiles going cheap that would match the avocado suite which we couldn't afford to change.

He was a master at making a little money go a long way. Without his handyman skills we'd be living in a derelict slum. Our home (the words still sent a warm tingle down my spine), was a wreck when we bought it. Wayne had worked non-stop to improve it.

In three months, our two-up-two-down terrace had been transformed from a soulless shell to a home and my heart swelled with pride and love whenever we had visitors dropping by.

"I'll get the shopping out, you put the kettle on," Wayne said, lifting six bags
Continued overleaf…

Cup of tea in hand, I opened the door – to a wonderful surprise

Continued from previous page

at once from the boot when we got home. As the kettle boiled, he stowed away the shopping then disappeared up the stairs with the last bag in his hand.

"Tea's ready," I shouted up the stairs ten minutes later.

"Can you bring it up, love?"

Mug of steaming tea in hand, I pushed open the bedroom door and gasped. Deep-red rose petals were strewn across the bed and cream candles on every spare surface flickered romantically. Wayne was crouching on one knee with his hand outstretched. In his fingers my "diamond" ring sparkled with a thousand lights.

"I'm sorry, Angie. I always meant to do this properly. I just got carried away in the fish aisle today," he said. "Angie, will you do me the great honour of agreeing to become my wife?"

Tears welled up. Never mind designer suits, shiny shoes and millionaires, Wayne's grubby clothes and paint-encrusted fingers were the marks of true love, for our home, our life – and me.

Clasping his hand in mine, holding back tears, I said, "I will."

He slipped the ring on to my finger and I turned it to and fro, watching it sparkle with a thousand lights and feeling its weight.

"One day I'll buy you a real diamond," he said, folding me into his strong arms.

I kissed him – a long, lingering kiss, full of love and passion. "Who needs real diamonds when you've got real love?" I said.

ABOUT THE AUTHOR

"Inspiration strikes during the most mundane tasks. With this story, it was at the checkouts"

Bright IDEAS!

Share your top tips and we can all save some time…

Cut off and keep the cooking instructions

Free Up Your Freezer

I always remove the cardboard packaging from frozen foods when I'm unpacking my shopping. This not only frees up space in my freezer, it also makes things a little quicker when it comes to cooking the food.
Fred Butler, Witton Gilbert

Tangle Free

I used to keep my silk scarves in a drawer but they were always getting tangled and creased. Now I loosely tie them onto a plastic coat hanger and keep them in my wardrobe. I can see which one I want to wear at a glance.
S Faulkner, Dunblane

No more creases

Clean In Comfort

I used to dread cleaning the oven as it was so uncomfortable on my knees. So I decided to buy myself a padded gardening cushion for kneeling on. The cushion can be wiped clean if it gets dirty and I can get on with the job in comfort!
Mary Green, Millom

Softer on the knees

Holiday At Home

Give your garden a Mediterranean look by adding a few potted cacti to your patio. They'll survive outdoors quite happily during the summer months and you'll feel as though you're somewhere hot and exotic, even if the weather lets you down!
Jane Bettany, Allestree

Surround yourself with cacti

Down To Earth

With A Bump

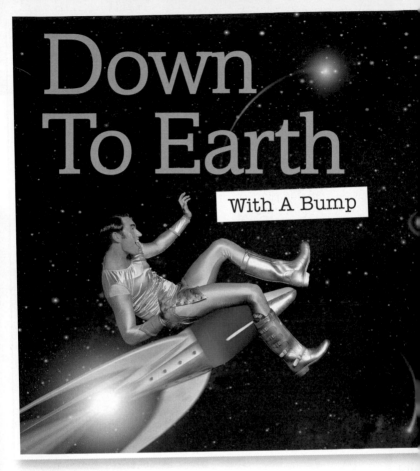

By Teresa Ashby

T here's a rip in the continuum," said Smith, running her fingers over the touch pad beside her screen following a hefty jolt that nearly knocked her out of her seat.

"That's impossible," Perkins said practically. "Try it again. You've probably just got a faulty oojamaflip in your dingbat."

"Are you all right, Perkins?" Smith turned to her senior officer. "You look a bit flushed."

"It's this new hormone advantagement nasal spray I've been using," Perkins complained. "I don't think it works. I've come over all unnecessary."

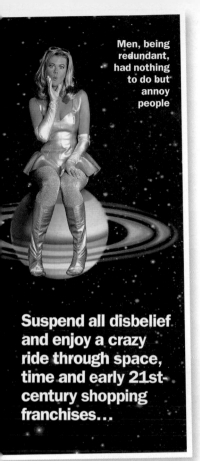

Men, being redundant, had nothing to do but annoy people

Suspend all disbelief and enjoy a crazy ride through space, time and early 21st-century shopping franchises…

Smith looked at her screen, she could see it was more than a mere tear. The entire fabric of space was coming apart.

Life as they knew it was likely to collapse into a black hole and never be the same again. The whole universe could be swallowed up – then what?

"Look at those spectra," Perkins breathed. "Beautiful, aren't they? – but they indicate a chasm of mega-proportions. I wonder what caused it?"

"Boy racers in their XJ1000 space cruisers, I shouldn't wonder," Smith said, shaking her head. It had been a bad day for humanity when all men were permanently retired from any of their duties and left entirely to their own devices.

With all of time on their hands, they had nothing to do but annoy people – female people, at any rate.

They were no longer required for any practical purpose and most weren't even aesthetically pleasing, but the humanity brigade wouldn't allow their extermination and so they remained a blight on society hanging round galaxies and generally making a nuisance of themselves.

"We have to repair that hole," Perkins said. "Any ideas, Smith?"

Smith shook her head. "We could ask Primark or Debenhams, maybe even Marks or Spencer – **Continued overleaf…**

She gave the small gold coloured cylinder a shake and squirted it up her nose.

"I'm not surprised it isn't working." Smith burst out laughing. "That's your allergen reducer! Aren't you supposed to spray it down your throat?"

But a hole in the continuum was no laughing matter and when

they work as a team."

"Ha! You might just as well ask McDonalds or Subway," Perkins muttered dismissively.

"Which ones?" Smith said. "There are so many of them."

"Well, it came to us all," Perkins sighed. "When Sir Ant and Dec found that bag factory on the old planet as they were filming *I'm An Alien Get Me Out Of Here*, the names printed on the bags became all the rage. There were four other Dorothy Perkins in my class at the academy and no less than six Peacocks. Professor Lidl used to get terribly confused."

"I've heard they're calling the latest batch of babies after stars," Smith said. "My new niece has been named Pishpai."

"Ah, how lovely," Perkins sighed. "Much better than being named after an old bag."

"Have you ever been to the old planet, Perkins?"

"Me? Oh, yes. I've been there and believe me, I wouldn't want to go back. Not ever."

"Was it really as bad as all that?"

Perkins face softened into a smile. "Well, not always I suppose. It had its good points. In all honesty I wouldn't change having been there, but I wouldn't want to go back there again… unless…"

She straightened her shoulders.

"No, I wouldn't want to go there again," she said. "Been there, done

that, got the scars to prove it as they say. But then again…"

"What's that?" Smith cried. "A vessel's approaching. Oh…"

The spacecraft swished across their bow. It was silver with a red nose cone, black go-faster stripe down one side and the name Burton splashed across the bow.

Coloured lights flashed through the tail fins and spoiler of the ship as it bobbed up and down in front of them. Music blared out. Smith could feel the beat of the music thrumming up through the floor of her patrol vessel.

"Pick up, cute stuff – I know you're in there." Burton's voice wafted through the sound vents. As always, he sounded so infuriatingly sure of himself.

"Cute stuff?" Smith spluttered.

"Better answer it, though." Perkins hid a smile. "See what he has to say for himself."

Smith opened a channel.

"What do you want, Burton?" she asked. "And make it quick, we have a situation here."

"I know." His face replaced the image of his ship on the big screen.

He was smiling. He had such white teeth. And dark eyes. Generally speaking, the males of the species left Smith cold, but Burton was a rare exception with his jet-black hair, deep brown eyes and expressive eyebrows.

Not that she'd ever noticed, mind you. She had better things to do than look with any more than the faintest wisp of curiosity at any infuriating men.

"It's more than a situation, W. H," he said, making Smith blush even more. "I'd say you're dealing with a catastrophe. That little old tear in the continuum is already the size of the Triangulum Galaxy and it seems to be growing."

nasal sprays. She used so many for different things that Smith was convinced she'd filled her head up with useless gas, leaving no room for sensible thought.

"Be my guest." Burton grinned and slowly his ship slid backwards leaving their path clear.

He was laughing at them. He knew they were flummoxed and he was enjoying every minute.

"So what now?" Smith hissed. "What do I do?"

"Don't ask me," Perkins giggled. "Ask him."

"But he's a . . . a *man*," Smith spluttered. "You know what they're like. He'll pretend to be interested in solving the problem, but all the time he'll be planning how to get me off to Betelgeuse where I'll be held captive and forced to iron space leggings and sweep space dust for the rest of my life."

"That's a myth," Perkins said

"It's more than a situation, W. H." She blushed. "I'd say it's a catastrophe"

He actually broke eye contact to inspect the tips of his fingernails. How cool was that?

"Then perhaps you'd like to get out of our way so that we can deal with it," Smith said sharply, coming back to her senses.

She wished Perkins would back her up, but she just stood there biting her lip. Drat her and her daft

reasonably. "There's no male-dominated planet anywhere near Betelgeuse. None in the entire universe since the Earth became uninhabitable, thanks to men! That's why we all have to live in a bubble on Mars when we're not patrolling space in our ships."

"It wasn't just us." Burton's voice **Continued overleaf...**

Continued from previous page

came through. "My great-grandfather told me that it was women and their hairspray and furniture polish who finally finished off the Earth."

"Hairspray and furniture polish?" Smith repeated. "What on earth are those?"

Perkins put her nasal spray in her pocket and shrugged. "Never heard of them," she said.

"And it's not a myth," Burton said. "There is a planet – we call it Earth Minor – where men and women live in perfect harmony. It's all natural, too – natural light, real water – not that reconstituted stuff you get from under Mars's crust – and we have flowers."

He said that with a hint of triumph in his voice. *Flowers.* The

"Ugh, now that sounds weird," Smith said. "Doesn't it sound weird to you, Perkins?"

But Perkins wasn't listening. "Tell me, Burton," she said. "Are

"I'll close the hole in the continuum with my remote control zapper"

very word sounded somehow magical to Smith.

"I've heard of those," Perkins said wistfully. "Men used to buy them for women when they wanted something or needed to apologise for some misdemeanour. Apparently they have a scent and come in a range of different colours and shapes."

"Women used to wear pictures of them on their clothing," Burton informed them smugly.

there older men on this Earth Minor? Say, my age?"

"Well there's House of Fraser, he's a nice chap," Burton replied. "And Recyclable Material, but he's getting ever so slightly shabby round the edges lately. Then there's Harrods, he's a bit aloof but a quality sort of bloke once you get to know him. Also Body Shop and Boots, regular guys."

"Boots?" Perkins came over all hot and had to sit down. "Not the

Smith had given up. There was a rapidly growing hole in the continuum and her commanding officer seemed to have taken leave of her senses. She'd always looked up to Perkins, always listened to her wise words, but now she was talking gobbledegook.

"Easy," Burton laughed. "Follow me – through the gap. It won't be open for long so you have to make up your minds."

"You mean it'll close on its own?" Smith perked up.

"No," Burton said. "I'll close it with my remote control zapper."

He demonstrated. The hole closed, the spectra vanished and the instruments on Smith's panel calmed down. She wasn't so sure she liked the sudden colourless void of space.

"Maybe men aren't so stupid," Smith said admiringly.

"Damn right we're not," Burton said. Somehow he was clutching her hand and she was sprawled out on her mother's sofa. And he wasn't Burton – he was Dan and she was Michelle.

"I only asked you to marry me. I didn't expect you to pass out."

"I've never seen anyone swoon before," Perkins said. "I didn't think girls actually did that sort of thing in real life."

"I didn't swoon," Michelle said. "The hole in the continuum closing up like that took me by surprise. **Continued overleaf…**

Boots who used to drive round space in a CRX convertible with headlights that winked?"

"The very same," Burton laughed. "He said if I ever ran into you I should say hello. You remember him then?"

"Remember him?" Perkins was having one of her flushes. She fanned her face with a laminated SA (Spaceship Association) route map to Sirius.

"So, how would we get to Betelgeuse – if we wanted to, that is?" Perkins asked, attempting to sound casual. "Being as it's four hundred light years from Old Earth which is that dark brown planet over yonder?"

The Earth rolled dimly in the sky. No longer a beautiful blue planet. Just another brown blob in the universe.

Continued from previous page

"She's delirious," Perkins said. "Just say yes, Michelle."

But it wasn't Perkins, it was her mum, Dot who had always said men were nothing but trouble. Judging by her excited smile, though, she seemed to have had a change of heart.

"I thought we were going shopping," Michelle murmured.

"We are," Dan laughed. "For a ring! If you'll say yes. Go on, cute stuff, make my day."

"Then yes." She smiled and the

What a wonderful day! A wedding to plan, and Boots was back in town

world was full of colour again.

Dot hugged them both.

She was still walking round with a smile on her face long after they'd left for the shops.

What a wonderful day. A wedding to plan, and the prospect of meeting up with Boots again (so called on account of the cowboy boots he used to wear back in the day).

He was back in town, footloose and fancy-free and it just so happened Dot was, too – footloose and fancy-free, that was.

She'd been off men for a while now – right off them – but that didn't mean she had to be off them for the rest of her life.

Never mind spending her

Saturdays sorting out her collection of carrier bags, which was what she was doing when Dan popped the question to Michelle – that was behind her now.

She may as well have been 400 light years from Earth these past few years, but not any more. Dorothy Perkins was back, and she was ready to live again.

ABOUT THE AUTHOR

"I love to read as much as I love to write. An all-time favourite book is *To Kill A Mockingbird*"

Stage fright

The Show Must Go On

The theatre audience are on the edge of their seats as tonight's performance becomes a spectral spectacle . . .

By Donald Lightwood

The theatre ghosts were tucked away amongst the beams and rafters under the roof.

"It's your turn," said Phyllis, the young soprano cut down by the postwar flu in 1919.

"No it's not," said Conrad, self-styled magician and prestidigitator, who knew a modest fame at the end of the 19th century.

"It is so," shouted out Hamish, a Scottish comic who had been carried off by drink.

"He's right," agreed Emily the contortionist, known as the Human Knot in the '20s.

Conrad groaned. "I was just getting comfortable," he told them, winding his way out of the fire bucket that had been his billet since the blitz.

Conrad passed through the floor of the roof space and the ceiling of the circle bar, and then through the wall into the auditorium. The show had started. On stage there was a man speaking to the audience through a microphone. Conrad snorted. They hadn't needed those contraptions in his day.

There was a silence. The man was holding his head in his hands, apparently concentrating very hard. At last he spoke. "Irene… I have a message for Irene… Is there an Irene here tonight?"

A woman in the audience jumped up. "My name's Irene," she cried.

The man spoke to her. "Irene, do you know anyone who has passed over recently?"

"My granny," she shouted back.

"And her name…?"

"Jean."

The man was still clasping his

Conrad and his fellow artistes could pass through walls and floors

Though he and his fellow artistes could pass through walls and floors, they could not see through them. And so to discover what was on at the theatre that evening, it was necessary for Conrad to go down to find out. The information he brought back would be chewed over with relish by the old stagers. They particularly enjoyed criticising pop groups.

head. "This is remarkable, truly remarkable. I am hearing a name very like that… It could be Joan… no, no, it's clearer now. It's, yes, it is… it's Jean."

There was a gasp from the assembled audience.

"And Jean has a message for you, Irene…"

In all his years in the business, Conrad had never come across an

act like this. The man had everybody in the palm of his hand. Evidently they knew what he was doing and were enjoying their night out at the theatre.

Conrad hung around for a little longer, but it was all the same sort of stuff. For a change he made his exit through the auditorium roof.

"No gags?" said Hamish, after Conrad had given his report.

"None whatsoever."

"It disnae make sense."

"Music hall has changed since our day," said Phyllis. "It must be some new kind of entertainment."

"Are there any other acts on the bill?" Emily asked.

"I didn't see anybody in the wings," Conrad told her. "The

amazing thing was how completely he held their attention."

"We can't expect to understand these modern changes, I suppose," Phyllis went on.

Conrad was puzzled. "This fellow has exactly the same task that we had. It's still live theatre, and with our experience we should be able to work out his trick."

"Just talking to the punters wi' no gags disnae seem all that clever to me," said Hamish.

Phyllis let out a sudden cry. "Somebody's calling out my name."

They all looked into the dusty corner where Milo, the ventriloquist usually lurked, but he wasn't there.

"There it is again!" Phyllis cried, this time with a giggle, as though she was being tickled. Then she disappeared.

"What curious behaviour," observed Conrad loftily.

The man on the stage was called Ivor Broadhurst and he was in full flight, with his head in his hands and an exultant expression on his round and shiny face.

"Yes… she's coming… I can feel her presence… Phyllis, do you have a message for your daughter?"

Phyllis hovered beside Ivor, trying to work out why she was there and what was going on.

"Can you hear me, dear? Phyllis… it's your daughter – here in the audience."

Phyllis looked out at the sea of **Continued overleaf…**

Continued from previous page
faces. It was the first time she'd been on the stage since her demise. A full house!

"Phyllis…?"

Did he know she was there? She knew nobody could see her. Was this man special in some way?

"Come along now… just a few small words…"

She didn't know how to communicate with him. Conrad had once talked about their being able to pass into living people if they wanted. It hadn't seemed like a nice idea to her, but maybe that's what she should do. She hovered closer and closer until suddenly she was part of him.

"I don't have a daughter," said Ivor, in Phyllis's voice.

There was an immediate response from the audience. Hearing him speak with a woman's voice surprised and thrilled them.

Ivor was even more surprised. It wasn't part of his routine. He knew some mediums spoke with spirit voices, but it had never happened to him. He had to readjust rapidly. There was laughter from the audience as someone shouted out that he'd got the wrong Phyllis.

"Do you have a message for anyone here?" said Ivor, thankful to find himself speaking in his own voice once more.

Phyllis stared out at the audience through the medium's eyes. Oh, the thrill of the spotlight picking her out centre stage! She nodded down to the orchestra pit and cast a glance up at the circle. And then she began to sing. "The boy I love is up in the gallery, The boy I love is waiting there for me."

Cries of astonishment greeted the pure soprano voice apparently coming out of Ivor. He himself stood as if transformed into a wax image of himself.

For him, spirits had been conjured not from the "other side", but from his ability to con people. He had been a charlatan all of his professional life. Something had gone seriously wrong.

"I sang – and they heard me," said Phyllis. Her companions listened in shocked silence. It was an accepted fact that they could neither be seen nor heard. "How?" demanded Emily.

"Like I said, I did my number through him."

"You're saying you did your act again?" said Hamish.

"Yes," she told him.

"That's brilliant!"

"To perform again," said Conrad. "It's unbelievable."

"Why didn't we know this was possible?" Emily asked him.

"Knowing what we can do has always seemed sufficient," Conrad shrugged. "Being invisible, passing through walls – it's extremely clever stuff. If I could have done that when I was on the halls, my magic act would have been world famous, I tell you."

"He called you?" said Hamish to Phyllis. "It seems he was trying to contact another Phyllis."

"By accident, as you have admitted," said Conrad. "Emily has a point. You've had your chance to do what we as artistes all crave. To perform again. Knowing that it is possible – albeit at secondhand – is the best news we've had since we passed over."

Things changed. Checking on the evening show was no longer one person's job. They all went down, each nurturing the hope of appearing on the stage once more.

A week later Ivor Broadhurst turned up again. Having discovered that he was on, the four spectral artistes hovered over the auditorium. It was packed.

Ivor himself was keyed up as never before. One half of him hoped he would attract a real spirit again, but the other half was

Phyllis hovered beside Ivor, trying to work out why she was there

"Why?" Phyllis asked.

"To answer questions, I think. He thought she was up here?"

"I've no idea," said Phyllis. "But if he calls again, I'll go."

"That wouldn't be fair," Emily responded hotly.

"What do you mean?"

"We should get a chance as well."

Phyllis pouted her lips. "It was me he called."

scared stiff. He knew he was taking a risk – exposing himself in full view of the public. However the possibility of fame and fortune urged him on.

Conrad soon became bored, listening to the man's chat and the inane questions from the audience. Having himself been in the business of deceiving people, he **Continued overleaf…**

Continued from previous page

recognised what Ivor was up to. As a magician, Conrad knew you could make people believe anything. It was obvious to him that the man was cheating – pretending to make contact with the spirit world. His "calling" Phyllis had clearly been accidental. Conrad was disappointed. How wonderful it would have been to form a bond with the living world through someone genuine!

He was shaken out of his musing by the man on stage. His voice had suddenly changed.

"Noo, you tak ma mither-in-law…" he said.

Conrad looked round. Hamish was missing.

"… and you can tak her whenever you want."

The audience was shocked into a stunned silence.

"That went better first house. Aye, ma mither-in-law – no kidding, she'd turn the milk sour. When she walks intae a room, the cat walks oot…"

Some people laughed, but mainly at the astonished expresson on Ivor's face. His hands went to his mouth in a vain attempt to silence himself.

"Did ye hear the one about the Englishman, the Irishman, and the Scotsman in the pub?" Hamish's voice went on. But then it suddenly stopped and Ivor found himself sitting on the stage. His legs began to wave about and incredibly it looked as if he was trying to wrap them round his neck.

It came as no surprise to Conrad that Emily, the Human Knot, was no longer beside him.

People were standing up out of their seats to get a better view. "He's possessed… he's flipped his lid… he's gone too far…"

Ivor was no youngster and had a modest pot belly, but even so, his legs locked themselves round his neck. Stuck as he was, unable to move any more, his voice suddenly came back.

"Whit the hell d'ye think you're up tae?" Hamish croaked out, somewhat higher than before. "I was just telling them one o' ma best gags there."

Ivor thrust his arms straight down and placed his palms on the stage. Then he moved his arms so that he was walking on his hands.

The audience went wild – though whether they were astonished at Ivor's skill, or felt aggrieved at the lack of spirit messages, was hard to tell.

It was obvious that he was cheating – pretending to contact the spirits

"Give us a song!" shouted a drunk, to a smattering of laughter.

Conrad didn't even bother to see if Phyllis was still at his side.

"No' you an' all..." complained Hamish's voice. It was topped by a bright soprano bursting into song.

"My old man said follow the van and don't dilly daily on the way..."

There was a thump. Ivor's arms had given way and the song ended. He had passed out and a stage manager ran on to the stage to untangle him.

By this time, there was consternation in the audience. The curtain came down and Conrad passed through it, as the theatre manager was pushing his way down the aisle to pacify his patrons.

Conrad hovered over the prone body of Ivor lying on the stage. It was evident that the other three had left him and gone aloft. The magician was not sorry for the calamity they had brought about. The man was a fraud and deserved to be unmasked. Conrad felt the urge to communicate this to him.

He slipped inside Ivor, who gave a shudder, and then began to speak in Ivor's voice.

"I am a fraud and have cheated innocent members of the public. I promise never to pretend to contact the spirit world again." Ivor nodded vigorously, and Conrad left him lying like a wet paperbag on the stage he had so grievously misused.

Satisfied, Conrad felt he had performed one of his better tricks. In the roof space a bitter argument was going on, as he settled down in his fire bucket. He sighed – nothing changed. There would always be people out to cheat the public, and for all their cheerful exterior, music hall artistes would always be jealous of each other – even when they were dead.

ABOUT THE AUTHOR

"Old theatres have always intrigued me. Showbusiness itself is a kind of magic and it seems natural to imagine the ghosts of music hall stars from the past."

Ladies' Night

Nancy decides she can't cope with being young again in this lively tale of new beginnings

By Jennifer Jordan

N ancy was beginning to feel just a little bit out of her comfort zone. Here she was, one sixty-something mother of the bridegroom-to-be, queuing to get into the trendiest nightclub in town with ten, highly excited, twenty-something girls.

Three months earlier, when Rosie had invited her, the idea of a hen night had sounded great fun but now, slowly shuffling along as the long line of chattering young people inched forward, doubts were very firmly settling in.

She paled slightly at the inflated price of the ticket but hadn't the courage to ask if there was a concession for pensioners. So, forcing a bright smile, she followed the girls into the dark, throbbing, stiflingly hot club. Already the pulsating music was far too loud for Nancy's delicate ears; was it her imagination or were the walls actually vibrating rhythmically in time to the loud music?

The pink fairy lights chasing each other manically around the bar made her squint for a moment as her eyes adjusted to the surrounding gloom. She didn't like the flickering laser lights either; she'd probably have one of her migraines tomorrow. But, determined to enjoy the evening, she smiled fondly at her daughter-in-law to be, pinned a frothy white veil to her hair and the 'hen' led the way to the cloakroom.

Nancy had agonised over what to wear. Her whole wardrobe these days consisted mainly of sensible, comfy clothes and wide fitting flat shoes. It had taken weeks to

Nancy watched a look of astonishment spread across her son's fiancée's face

She followed the girls into the dark night club

choose an outfit suitable for a hen night. If only Jean had been able to come too they could have given each other advice on what to wear, but Rosie's mother lived three hundred miles away in Cornwall.

"Come on, Mum-in-law, you must be boiling hot in that coat." Rosie's smile was gentle.

Continued overleaf…

Continued from previous page

Nancy slowly and shyly took off her long beige coat and watched a look of pure astonishment spread across her son's fiancée's face.

Maybe I shouldn't have worn such a tight skirt, thought Nancy uncomfortably. Nervously she fiddled with her strappy top, startled for a moment by the sight of her own generous cleavage, considerably enhanced by the Bumper Busty Booster Bra. Discreetly she checked the tops of her stockings; they had been a complete impulse buy. She had ignored her usual beige support tights and, smiling wryly at the memory of the sturdy, serviceable girdles of her youth, was unable to resist these glossy black wisps of stockings with lacy stretchy tops. They had looked so pretty on the mannequin in the department store. Nancy's legs were shorter

heels, trailed hesitantly behind and willed her body to move fluidly with the music as she had done years ago, but her limbs felt stiff and awkward and as old as the hills. The pounding jungle rhythm of the drums hammered relentlessly at her senses, the flashing lights startling her when they sliced through the gloom.

She nailed a smile to her face, intent on enjoying herself, as the evening wore slowly on. Nearly three long, exhausting hours later, she sneaked a discreet look at her watch and couldn't help thinking that she would normally be cosily tucked up for the night by now; snuggled into Harry's warm back in their big, comfy bed.

The karaoke started just as Nancy was fighting her way back from the cloakroom. "And now!" boomed the DJ, "Anyone remember the sixties?"

Relief flooded sweetly through her; at last it was time to go home to bed

and sturdier than the mannequin's but she didn't care; she felt feminine and totally gorgeous.

"Follow us, Mum-in-law!" Rosie and the girls, their spirits as high as their hemlines, soon boogied their way into the middle of the heaving dance floor.

Nancy, teetering on her high

"Yes, I do," Nancy heard herself saying. Suddenly, someone escorted her up on to the stage, her stilettos tip-tapping on the wooden floor. Then the music throbbed into life and panic seized her as she looked at the sea of young faces gazing expectantly up at her. Someone handed her a microphone and the words began

to tumble one after another across the karaoke screen.

Let's twist again! Like we did last summer! Nancy could just about read the lyrics without her specs and slowly began to relax, enjoying herself now as she belted out the familiar songs of her youth. Forty minutes later, after giving it all she had, she gave a sweeping theatrical bow and smiled delightedly at the whistles, cheers and resounding applause.

"Come on, Mum-in-law," grinned Rosie, helping her down from the stage. "The minibus is waiting for us outside."

Nancy couldn't ever remember feeling so hot, so fatigued or so exhilarated. Smudges of mascara edged her tired eyes, both heels were painfully blistered and the Bumper Busty Booster Bra was slightly askew from both its occupants. The left hold-up stocking had slithered to her knee and the right one was clinging on for dear life. But relief flooded sweetly through her; at last it was time to go home to bed.

"We're going on to another club now," explained a bright-eyed Rosie excitedly.

"Another club?" Nancy looked at the girls in complete astonishment. "Whatever for? Weren't you happy with this one?"

"Yes, we loved it," laughed Rosie, "But it's not late, it's only half past midnight."

"But aren't you all exhausted?"

"No, of course not." Rosie put an arm around Nancy's shoulders. "But if you really are too tired, we'll drop you off at home."

"Well, I am ready for bed," agreed Nancy, not wishing to be a party-pooper, but the thought of a soft nightie and a hot, soothing, creamy cup of cocoa was just too hard for her to resist.

Waving at the departing minibus, Nancy removed her high heels, tiptoed along the garden path and stood for a moment allowing the soft, cool night air to caress her flushed face before sliding her key in the lock. **Continued overleaf…**

Continued from previous page

Harry was obviously sound asleep; the bungalow was eerily silent as she slipped inside, fumbling in the darkness. The microwave clock gently glowed in the kitchen, casting a dim light on the cat who snuggled further into her basket, grunting gently at being disturbed.

Padding down the hall to peer around the bedroom door, the shrill, urgent chirrup of the telephone shattered the silence.

"Mum? I've been trying to ring you for ages."

Nancy gripped the phone, a cold chill of panic sweeping over her as she heard her son's anxious voice.

"What's wrong, Steven?"

"Dad's at the hospital."

Nancy barely heard the rest. "Digging the allotment… chest pains… ambulance."

With shaking hands, she called a local taxi to take her to the hospital immediately.

Harry was sleepy and looked small and pale in the big hospital bed. He'd had lots of tests, the young nurse told her. Nancy held her husband's limp hand and clutched Steven's arm, willing herself to stay calm.

"How is he?" She struggled to speak through dry lips.

"We'll know soon enough, Mum."

They both sat, deep in their own thoughts, watching the nurse busying herself around the bed. The clock ticked; other patients in the small ward snuffled and snored while Nancy trembled gently on her hard, cold, hospital chair.

Suddenly the curtains parted and the doctor, who looked about fourteen, appeared. "Tests are all fine," he announced, cheerfully. "But he's torn a muscle rather badly in his chest."

"Can he come home?" Nancy was still wobbling slightly.

"Yes, tomorrow. We've given

Nancy leant for a moment against Steven's comforting warmth

Nancy realised that she was wearing her pink, fluffy slippers with her coat

him a sedative for tonight."

Nancy gently kissed her sleeping husband and then leant for a moment against Steven's comforting warmth as he hugged her. It was then that she realised that she'd grabbed the first available pair of shoes and was wearing her pink, fluffy, pussycat slippers with her long beige coat.

O h, it's so good to be home." Harry stretched luxuriously and then grimaced as he felt the sharp stab of his torn muscle. "But I do feel extremely ancient. How I'd love to be young again, wouldn't you, love?"

Nancy, perched precariously on the edge of the bed, looked thoughtfully at her hen night outfit slung carelessly over the wardrobe door, the patent stilettos leaning tipsily together on the floor.

"No," she said, with conviction, "I really don't think I could cope with being young again!"

Harry was quiet for a moment. "This could have been a lot more serious," he said, solemnly

pointing to his chest, "It's made me think. Why don't we book a super holiday and go away while Steven and Rosie are off on their honeymoon together?"

Nancy planted a soft kiss on her husband's forehead. "Great idea," she smiled, her voice bright with excitement, "but I do have one condition."

"What's that then?"

"That the hotel must have a karaoke bar."

Harry groaned and clutched his head in mock despair. "Well I've got a condition too," he said, looking at her boldly.

"What's that then?"

"That you don't wear those stockings again."

"But… but I thought I looked a tiny bit glamorous!" protested Nancy, trying very hard to hide her bruised feelings.

"You did, my darling," Harry's blue eyes twinkled, "But I dug twenty pounds of onions on the allotment. I think those stockings are just perfect for them – they'd store in there a treat!"

ABOUT THE AUTHOR

Jennifer often gets inspiration for her stories from snippets of gossip in the village shop!

Like A Penny Candle...

Be touched by this emotional tale of one woman's journey to find a flicker of light in her life after she loses someone she loves...

A flickering light of hope

By Paula Williams

Jenna watched as her mother, Helen, lit the tall red candle then picked up the baby and held him towards the flickering light. As his forget-me-not eyes widened at the sight of the dancing flame Helen smiled down at him and began to sing softly.

"Jesus bids us shine with a clear, pure light,

Like a penny candle, burning in the night…"

"No. Please stop." Jenna knocked over her chair in her anxiety to get away.

But it was too late. The little song, and all the pain-filled memories it evoked was lodged firmly inside her head.

Her anguished cry and sudden movement startled the baby and

his small face puckered, ready for tears. Helen soothed him by stroking his downy head with cool, practised fingers while she looked anxiously across at her daughter.

"Jenna? Are you all right?" she asked gently.

As Jenna turned to answer, she intercepted the worried look that passed between her husband and her mother.

"Of course I am." Her voice was sharper than she'd intended but it was the best she could do. She was having difficulty getting it under control at all. "Sorry. I didn't mean … it's just – that song…" She

they'd leave her alone.

"I'll put Lucas back in his cot, shall I?" Helen said softly. "He's nearly asleep again, bless him. Unless you'd like to…?"

Jenna shook her head without turning round, not wanting to see the pain and worry that she knew would be clouding her mother's eyes in that moment.

"Jenna, please…" Dan began gently as Helen left the room with the baby. "Your mother's grieving too, you know."

"I know. I know," she cried. "And I hate myself for being like this. But it isn't…oh, it's hopeless. I just

His forget-me-not eyes widened at the sight of the dancing flame

swallowed hard, then shook her head to indicate she couldn't go on.

"…is what your dad used to sing to you." Helen finished the sentence for her. "'I know." She sighed deeply and a shadow crossed her face. "But don't you think it would be nice for Lucas to grow up hearing the same things you did as a child?"

"But they won't be the same, though, will they?" The familiar surge of hard, cold anger churned her insides. "Because it'll be you singing them, not him."

She turned away before either of them could see the tears in her eyes and wished with all her heart

can't explain how I feel."

"Would you like a word with the doctor again?"

"And tell him what?" She scowled at him, "That I can't bond with my baby? Or I can't come to terms with my father's death? Isn't that the jargon?"

Or, she added silently to herself, should I tell him the truth? The thing that's eating me up inside? Something so dreadful, I'm ashamed to tell anyone. Even Dan.

What would he say if I told him that not only do I resent the fact Mum was with Dad when he died and I wasn't but I resent the baby, **Continued overleaf…**

Continued from previous page
too, for keeping me away from going to Dad at that time?

For in one of fate's cruellest twists, little Lucas Sanders came in to the world ninety-two minutes before his grandfather, John, left it.

Both events had been earlier than expected. Lucas arrived by emergency Caesarean section four weeks sooner than he should have done and John's cancer specialist had been quietly optimistic that John would live long enough to see his first grandchild.

But it was not to be. There'd been complications following her Caesarean and as Jenna came round from the anaesthetic, Dan was by the side of her bed, ashen faced. He told her that, half an hour after the birth of their beautiful baby boy, her father had slipped into unconsciousness and an hour later had quietly died.

That was seven weeks ago. Seven weeks of missing him so

Dan patted the space on the sofa next to him.

For a moment, she remained standing at the window. She knew it was stupid but every time she looked into the garden, she still expected to see her father bent over a flower bed, humming one of his silly songs to himself as he did so.

But the garden was silent and empty, filled only with the lengthening evening shadows as the light faded and a solitary blackbird singing in the apple tree.

She dragged herself away and went to sit beside Dan. "Poor Mum, I shouldn't have… you're quite right, of course. I keep forgetting she's lost him as well. I'm so selfish. I can't…"

Her voice stumbled over the words. Dan put his arm around her shoulder and pulled her towards him. At first, she resisted, but he held her close and gradually she relaxed in to him and buried her face in his chest.

The pain had become physical, a deep ache she carried with her everywhere

much the pain had become physical, a deep ache she carried with her everywhere.

Seven weeks, too, of the shameful resentment towards her beautiful baby that she dared not put into words.

"Jenna, come and sit down."

Then, for the first time since her father died she began to cry. Deep, painful sobs that shook her body and exhausted her until, at last, there were no more tears.

"Jenna." Helen had come back downstairs after putting Lucas to bed. At a nod from Dan, she took

face when he saw it – well, it all made a sort of sense to me. You know, how when you light a candle in a dark room, nothing happens for a while? Then gradually the light from the candle spreads right across the room, even in to the darkest corners?"

Jenna nodded as she looked across at the tall red candle, still shining on the mantelpiece, its soft flickering sending tiny rainbows of light dancing off the glass vase sitting next to it.

"That's how I feel about Lucas," Helen said. "When your father first died, everything was black. So very black. But then there was Lucas, like a little penny candle. At first, there was hardly any light but with every day that passes, his light becomes stronger. There are still many, many dark corners in my room, and I suspect they'll be there for some time, but as Lucas gets bigger, so his light will grow. Let him shed some of his light in to your dark corners, Jenna. He will if you decide to let him."

Jenna's hand. "I didn't mean to upset you with Penny Candle and…"

"Mum, I'm sorry. I really shouldn't have…"

"Hear me out. I want to explain why I was singing it. Your dad had such a huge repertoire of songs, didn't he? Some dafter than others. I still think he made half of them up, though he swore his father used to sing them." She gave a short, forced laugh. "I mean, whoever would write a song called *Where's my other Flipping Sock?*? Remember that one? Or what about *I'm a Lonely Little Petunia in an Onion Patch*?"

Jenna nodded as she remembered, an unwilling smile tugging at the corner of her mouth.

"I read something a couple of weeks ago that helped me a bit," Helen went on, heartened by the first sign of a loosening of the tension in her daughter's too-pale face. "And just now, when I lit the candle and watched little Lucas's

After that day, things started to improve. Whether it was the healing power of her tears or her mother's theory about candles, Jenna wasn't sure. But gradually she began to feel better about the baby and the resentment that had sat in her chest like a lump of ice began to melt away.

Continued overleaf…

But still she'd intercept worried glances between Dan and her mother and she challenged Dan about it one bright September morning, two weeks before Lucas's first birthday.

"What is it?" she asked when her mother had gone. "Why are you and Mum still fretting so much about me? I'm fine now really. Surely you can see that?"

"Of course. It's just that…" Dan took her hands, his eyes full of loving concern. "You've lost your sparkle, my love. You used to be so full of life, always singing around the place, so like…"

"So like my father. That's what you mean, isn't it? But, don't you see? I'm just not that person any more. Inside, a bit of me died the day he did, I suppose."

And I can't find him, she added silently. She couldn't tell Dan about all the time she'd spent trying to do so because it wasn't rational.

Her mother coped with her grief by reliving happy memories and, of course, there was Lucas and the candle light.

But that didn't work for Jenna. She loved her small son to bits and he certainly helped fill the gaping hole in her life. But there was still an emptiness inside her that wouldn't be completely filled unless she could "find" her father.

Not long before he died, on the terrible day he'd told her there was to be no more chemotherapy, she'd broken down completely and had begged him not to leave her. He'd taken her hand in his and looked deep into her eyes.

"I'll never leave you," he'd said, "After I'm gone, you'll find me again, I promise. Because I'll always be with you."

But that was the one promise he'd been unable to keep.

Jenna had looked everywhere for him – the cemetery, the football ground, the park where he walked the dog. Nothing. But she kept looking, although she'd no idea what she was looking for – only, she hoped, that she'd know it when she saw it. Like her mother

He was everywhere, filling all the dark corners of her life with light

and the little penny candle.

On Lucas's first birthday and the anniversary of John's death, Dan suggested they all went to Lyme Regis. "I thought it would be good to remember your dad in one of his favourite places," he said.

She was touched by his thoughtfulness, but the day was not a success. Helen came with them and, in spite of their attempts not to be, their mood was as sombre as the weather. Even at Lyme, a place so full of happy memories of him and the many holidays they'd spent there, Jenna had failed to find him.

It was late when they got home. Jenna put Lucas down on the floor with one of his new toys while she went in to the kitchen to prepare his supper. When she came back in to the room, Helen and Dan were watching him intently.

"Look," Helen whispered, "He's trying to puzzle out which bit goes where – and look, he…"

"Looks just like Dad." Jenna's heart skipped a beat as she looked at her baby son and found what she'd spent so long looking for. Lucas was frowning as he puzzled over his new toy. His head was bent forward, his tongue sticking out as he concentrated. He was…

"The image of his grandfather," Helen murmured, her eyes shimmering with tears. "Can't you see it, darling?"

Jenna nodded, not trusting herself to speak, overwhelmed with love for her young son and for her father who still lived on in Lucas's frown, in the way his tongue was caught between his teeth.

Of course he lived on. Jenna had simply been looking in all of the wrong places.

After that she saw her father everywhere – in the lovely wrought iron arch he'd built for her garden; in her brother who looked so much like him; in her baby son, who frowned and chewed his tongue as he concentrated.

He was in the stars he'd taught her to recognise and the silly songs he'd sang that still danced through her head at inappropriate moments. He was in the birds he'd named for her and the music he'd taught her to love.

He was in her heart. He was everywhere, filling all the dark corners of her life with light. Just like the little Penny Candle.

"In this world of darkness, so we must shine,
You in your small corner, and I in mine."

ABOUT THE AUTHOR

My inspiration is my dad, who'd stick out his tongue slightly when concentrating. When I saw my grand-daughter doing the same thing, I had to write about it

Tears, Fears Eccles Cake

Andrea's struggle to understand her teenage
daughter's moods will have you smiling in sympathy...

By Linda March

i, Mum? It's me. Is Kirsty
there? Oh, thank
goodness. Send her
home, will you?
Preferably with a flea in her ear!"

That's how it had all started,
Andrea reflected. It seemed that
her daughter, Kirsty, had just
woken up one morning a couple of
months ago and decided to
become a teenager. And, at only
12, this was a bit ahead of schedule
as far as Andrea was concerned.
So she had been completely taken
aback by the reaction she got when
she tossed a new pair of tights on
the kitchen table as Kirsty came in
from school that afternoon.

"Grey tights?"

"Yes, they're lovely and soft and

they'll be cosy on chilly mornings,"
Andrea said as she filled the kettle.

"Grey tights?" Kirsty repeated in
disbelief. "Nobody at school wears
grey tights, not one single person!"

"I find that hard to believe since
they're on the school uniform list."

"Huh! Nobody bothers with that
stuff any more."

"Well, I do."

"Yeah, you would, of course"
Kirsty muttered.

"What on earth's that supposed
to mean?"

"Nothing." The response was
little more than a grunt.

"What on earth's got into you
today?" Andrea asked. "It's only a
pair of tights."

"That shows how much you
know." Kirsty snorted.

"Well, what I do know is that

Kirsty had woken up one morning and decided to become a moody teenager

you'll be wearing them to school tomorrow," Andrea told her firmly. "Now, go and hang up your coat."

"I'm not wearing them!" The look was mutinous and Kirsty all but stamped her foot.

"Yes you are, young lady!"

"You don't understand anything!" and with a furious scowl Kirsty slammed the door shut behind her.

Andrea took a while to take in what had just happened. Had her normally sunny-tempered daughter really just stormed out of the house over a pair of grey tights? It was ridiculous. She and Kirsty never argued. Widowed when Kirsty was still a toddler, Andrea had built a life for the two of them into which very few drops of discord fell.

Everyone said that Kirsty was the spitting image of her mother at **Continued overleaf…**

that age: long legged, sandy haired and fine boned. And they were alike in so many ways; they even shared many of the same interests. They rubbed along together so well, it was unthinkable that a mere pair of tights should have caused such ructions.

Pouring herself a cup of tea, Andrea sat down at the kitchen table and waited for Kirsty's return. Best thing was to ignore her daughter's outburst and just pretend it had never happened. Least said soonest mended.

Reflecting on the earlier scene, she cringed at the memory of her retort – "Yes you are, young lady!" Had she really said that? It was the

that Kirsty was indeed there.

"I think our Kirsty's beginning to grow up," Andrea's mother, Sylvia, said gently.

"Maybe," Andrea agreed. "But that's no excuse for storming out of the house over a pair of tights!"

"Sometimes it's the smallest things that lead to the biggest quarrels, you know."

Now, two months on, there seemed to be fewer and fewer glimpses of her daughter's happy smiling face and Andrea was almost growing used to sulks and grunts over the dining table. Not that Kirsty had shown her face, sulky or otherwise, tonight. For the second time this week she'd not

Andrea was almost growing used to her sulks and grunts over the dining table

kind of comment that your own mother had made and that you promised yourself you would never repeat. Well, that was parenthood for you.

After her second cup of tea, Andrea glanced up at the clock. An hour and a half had passed and worriedly, she began telephoning Kirsty's many friends. No joy. Anxiety starting to take hold, she wondered whether Kirsty was holed up at her grandmother's house.

Andrea dialled the number and was extremely relieved to discover

come straight home from school. No prizes for guessing where she was. Irritated, Andrea picked up the phone.

"Dad? It's me. Oh, she is, is she? Well, she knows she's supposed to come home first to let me know where she's going." There was an edge to Andrea's voice. "Would you send her home straight away please? Tell her I'm about to get dinner ready."

Andrea could hear her father calling Kirsty and her daughter's voice in the distance. Then the receiver had obviously been covered up because the line went completely silent. Andrea exhaled heavily. Really, she thought, there was nothing to discuss. Her father should just tell Kirsty to go home now.

"Andrea?" It was her mother's voice. "Hello, love. Would it be all right if Kirsty stayed a while longer? It's just that we're in the middle of something and…"

"In the middle of what?" Andrea interrupted rather abruptly.

"Baking a cake for the church fundraiser," Sylvia explained. "Kirsty wants to stay and help decorate it."

"I don't know, Mum," Andrea said crisply. "I was about to start dinner, and then there's her homework."

"Oh she's finished her homework," Sylvia assured her. "I made sure she got that done first. And I've plenty of shepherd's pie to do Kirsty. You know your father says I always make enough to feed the street," she laughed. "Your dad'll drop her home right after we've eaten."

Andrea put down the phone, having agreed to Sylvia's request.

It would have been churlish not to, but she wasn't happy. Her mother seemed to see more of Kirsty than she did these days. Putting the ingredients for the bolognese sauce back in the fridge, she sighed. It really wasn't worth cooking for one. She'd just make herself a sandwich.

As she chopped salad, Andrea felt the niggle of annoyance grow. It had been safely established that the only thing ailing Kirsty was adolescent angst. A telephone call to Kirsty's form teacher had confirmed that, as far as the school was concerned, there were no problems with her work or her schoolmates. If she was anything less than the polite and charming girl she usually was, they simply put it down to her age.

"Tell me about it!" Hannah's mother, Karen, had retorted when Andrea described the sullenness and bursts of temper which seemed to come out of nowhere. "Hannah's the same. Slammed her bedroom door so hard she broke a mirror last week. Serve you right, I thought to myself, until she started wailing about seven years' bad luck. I thought we'd never hear the end of it."

"Well, I'm relieved it's nothing more than an age thing," Andrea admitted. "I just hope it doesn't last too long."

Continued overleaf…

Continued from previous page

"A mere five or six years probably," Karen grimaced. "But I suppose we were exactly the same at their age."

"Never!" Andrea grinned, but it made her think.

So if it were nothing more than teenage blues, Kirsty, along with everyone else, was just going to have to learn to cope with it. And Andrea really thought her mother might have been more supportive, rather than pandering to Kirsty's every whim and giving in to her all the time. It was hard enough for Andrea to maintain some sense of discipline without Kirsty feeling she could run to Grandma every time things didn't suit her.

Take tonight for instance. Kirsty was allowed to go to the park or to a friend's house before dinner. But the rule was that she came straight home from school first. That way Andrea always knew where she was. Tonight Kirsty had broken the rules, and instead of being sent home, she was rewarded by being allowed to stay longer and have dinner at Grandma's.

"Ouch!" The knife slipped off the end of the tomato she was

slicing. That's what happened when you weren't concentrating. Andrea gently ran cold water over her cut finger. The trouble was, she was finding it hard to concentrate on anything other than Kirsty. She must keep things in perspective. She needed a project to take her mind off things.

"I know," she said aloud, turning off the tap and drying her hands. "I'll make those curtains for the back bedroom."

She'd bought the pretty patterned fabric and lining material in the sales last year, but since then it had been stowed in the blanket chest in her bedroom. She'd get it out tonight and make a start.

She soon discovered that the curtain-making project was enough to keep her mind occupied. The fabric was trickier to work with than she'd imagined and she'd rather rashly chosen a complicated pleat design that she'd seen in a magazine for the curtain tops.

A fairly proficient needlewoman, well taught by her mother, she had thought the project within her capabilities, but by the fourth day of struggling, she knew she'd have to call in the big guns or risk making such a hash of things that the fabric would be spoiled and wasted. Luckily, she knew just the person for the job.

"Mum? It's me." In her youth Sylvia had trained as a curtain and upholstery maker with one of the big department stores in town. Then, once Andrea and her brothers had come along, she'd worked freelance from home, fitting in sewing jobs around busy family life. Although she did less these days, she still kept her hand

agitated, her stomach churning. Finally, grabbing her coat, she made for the door. She knew where to go, and a glance at the clock told her she just had time before Kirsty came home from school.

It took Andrea's grandmother a few minutes to answer the door these days, but at 84, and otherwise hale and hearty, a little stiffness in the legs was to be expected, according to Dr. Simons.

She was finding it hard to concentrate on anything other than Kirsty

in with orders from friends and neighbours.

"Oh love, I'm sorry," Sylvia said when Andrea explained the problem. "I can't do anything at the moment; I'm up to my ears. I will help, of course, but it'll be a couple of weeks before I've got time. Sorry, darling."

Andrea felt a surge of resentment. "I quite understand if you're too busy, Mum," she said curtly. "Perhaps if my name was Kirsty it'd be different…"

"Andrea love," Sylvia began, but Andrea, feeling hurt, finished the conversation abruptly.

"Must go, Mum. I'm busy, too, you know. 'Bye."

Returning to the kitchen, she filled the kettle, but as it boiled she paced the floor, restless and

"It might be what you expect," May Samuels had told him, "but I don't really have time for stiff legs and suchlike."

"It's just life's way of telling you to slow down, May," the doctor had smiled.

"Well, life will have to shout louder. I'm not listening."

"Oh no, here comes trouble," May said when she found her granddaughter standing on the doorstep with a paper bag from the village bakery. "Those had better be Eccles cakes."

"Of course, Gran," Andrea grinned, closing the front door behind her. "I know better than to come here without Eccles cakes. Shall I get the kettle on?"

When they were settled **Continued overleaf…**

Continued from previous page

comfortably in the sunny lounge of her little bungalow, May asked how Kirsty was.

"Just the same. I can't say anything right. Everything turns into a drama and she flies off the handle at the slightest thing."

"You know how girls are at that age. You can't tell them anything. They have to find everything out for themselves."

"I try to bite my tongue, but we've had a couple of humdinger rows, Gran," Andrea admitted.

"Over the smallest things too, I'll bet. That's the way of it."

Andrea nodded at her grandmother's wise words. "You'll just have to ride it out, my girl," May said. "Take a stand on the things that really matter and let the little things go. She'll grow out of it." She took a sip of tea. "Eventually."

"Just hope I survive."

"No one's died from having a teenage daughter yet," May smiled knowingly.

"There's always a first time," Andrea said glumly, draining her cup in one gulp.

"You sure there's not more bothering you than our teenage drama queen?" May looked closely at her granddaughter.

Andrea shook her head.

"Sure?"

There was silence for a moment and then the

words came tumbling out.

"Well, it doesn't help that whenever she's not happy with something I've said or done, Kirsty runs to Mum. Honestly, she spends more time there than at home."

"Does that matter?"

"I think Mum should be more supportive, back me up when Kirsty's flounced out. But she just rewards her by giving her more time and attention."

"Maybe that's what Kirsty needs at the moment."

"Spoiling, you mean?"

"Not spoiling. Loving."

"Are you saying I don't love her?" Andrea's eyes were wide with indignation.

"Of course not. You're a wonderful mother." May patted her granddaughter's hand. "Sylvia and I were so worried about how you'd cope when Colin died, but you've really made us proud. No one could have done more for Kirsty, but these in-between years are difficult. She's trying things out and finding her feet.

"If I can remember that far back, I'm sure a young thing like you can! Perhaps she just needs a little bit more love than only one person

can give at the moment."

"So she turns to Mum?"

May nodded. Andrea sighed deeply. She supposed it made sense. But…

"But what about me?" she blurted out in a hurt voice.

"You?"

"Mum's got all the time in the world for Kirsty, but when I need her it's a different story." And she told May about the curtains.

"Sylvia's certainly busy at the moment, had a couple of big orders in. I think you're reading too much into this, dear."

Three sharp rings on the doorbell prevented any reply.

"Fine."

"That's good."

"Well, no, not really, Mum. I think I've upset Andrea."

"Oh dear." As May pushed open the door to the kitchen, her daughter and granddaughter looked first surprised, and then annoyed, to see one another.

"Oh. I might I have guessed you'd be straight round here," Sylvia said snippily.

"What do you mean?"

"Well, it was always the same when you were young. As soon as I said or did something you didn't like, you flounced off to your grandmother's."

"No one's died from having a teenage daughter yet," May smiled

"I'll go, Gran," Andrea offered.

"No, no, got to keep these legs moving," May sighed as she heaved herself out of the chair. "Let them know who's boss. You put the kettle on again."

A figure, slightly shorter than Andrea, with the same grey blue eyes, stood on the doorstep, holding a village bakery bag.

"Hello, Mum. Got time for a cup of tea and a cake?"

"If I said no, Sylvia, you wouldn't believe me." May preceded her daughter down the hall. "Everything all right, dear?"

"Leave me out of this," May said, unpacking the cakes.

"I did not!" Andrea protested.

"Yes you did. When you were Kirsty's age, I couldn't say or do anything right. You'd take umbrage and be straight round to Grandma's, so that she could spoil you with cakes."

May's lips twitched and there was a twinkle in her eye as she spoke. "No wonder none of us is a size ten. It's all my fault!"

"Oh Gran," Andrea sighed. "What are we like? Talk about history repeating itself."

Continued overleaf…

Continued from previous page

"What on earth do you mean?" asked Sylvia.

"Andrea was just saying that she never sees Kirsty these days," May explained. "She's always round at her grandmother's."

"Getting spoiled," Andrea added with a grin as she filled the teapot.

"Oh," Sylvia gave a long sigh. "Oh I see. I am sorry, love," she said, touching her daughter's shoulder. "I didn't mean to step on your toes. I just wanted to be there for Kirsty if she needed me."

"No, I'm sorry for being such a… teenager over it," Andrea said, giving Sylvia a hug. "We all need a bolt-hole sometimes and I should have been grateful that Kirsty had someone else to turn to. Just like I did," she added, smiling at her grandmother. "Though my hips could probably have done without so many Eccles cakes."

"Well, when you're a grandmother, you can spoil your grandchildren with healthy fruit snacks," May told her. "My, we're popular today," she added as the doorbell rang again.

This time a much younger version of the grey blue eyes was standing at the door.

"Hi Gran-Gran," Kirsty said. "Can I come in? Mum's not home and nor is Gran."

"'Course you can! In you come, dear," May said, smiling.

When Kirsty walked into the kitchen and saw her mother and grandmother, her face broke into the kind of beaming smile that seemed to have become a distant memory recently.

"Oh, cool. You're all here."

"Yes, Kirsty," Andrea said. "We're all here for you." And as she looked round the kitchen at four generations of women, she knew how lucky they were to have each other. Minor quarrels would come and go – that was family life – but the love and support would always be there.

"I'm starving," Kirsty said, her eyes roaming the room. "Aren't there any cakes?"

The Lost Ticket

This cheeky tale of a long-suffering young wife who takes matters into her own hands is sure to raise a chuckle

Farewell sadness, hello happiness

By Margaret Skipworth

Della cast an apologetic glance at Ryan, her husband. "I'm sure I put it in my bag."

"I should've known better than to trust you with your ticket." Ryan sighed irritably and glared at her.

The airport official cleared his throat. "Perhaps if you went through the contents of your handbag… Your ticket might have slipped in between something else." He smiled sympathetically. "We can go somewhere private to look for it if you prefer."

Della looked at the man's badge. His name was Bob. A good solid, **Continued overleaf…**

Continued from previous page

reliable name, she thought. She smiled her thanks.

"Can we get on with this?" Ryan snarled. "We've a plane to catch, in case you'd forgotten."

Bob led Della and Ryan to a small room and closed the door behind them. Ryan slumped into a chair while Della poured the contents of her bag on to a table in the centre of the room.

Ryan rolled his eyes in exasperation. "It's just like you to mess things up, Della. I don't know why my sister wanted you at her wedding anyway. I mean, you're not exactly mates or…"

Della stopped listening. She found it easy to switch off. She'd become an expert at shutting out Ryan's tantrums during the five years they'd been married. If only Ryan knew the significance of some of these items on the table, she thought wryly as she carefully sifted through them.

There was a bottle of expensive French perfume. Della couldn't help smiling as she remembered the three wonderful days she'd spent in Paris. Normally Ryan wouldn't let her out of his sight, let alone out of the country without him. But her mother had been going to France on a business trip

The voice had a thick French accent that sent a tingle down Della's spine

and had asked Della to accompany her. There was no way Ryan could refuse without appearing churlish.

She picked up a lipstick. Deep purple. If she hadn't removed the label, Ryan would have noticed it wasn't the pinky-peach shade he always insisted she wore.

"You won't find your ticket in that lipstick." Ryan's voice dripped with contempt. Della ignored him as she rolled the lipstick comfortingly between her fingers.

Ryan stabbed a finger at his watch. "Look at the time. We're going to miss the plane."

"I can't let you on the plane without a ticket." Bob's eyes were full of concern

Della gave a small shrug. "Sorry," she told Bob, "I must have left my ticket at home."

"I can't let you on the plane without a ticket." Bob's soft brown eyes were full of concern.

"Can I buy another ticket?" Della asked, scooping up her belongings and stuffing them in her bag.

"I'm afraid the plane's full," Bob said. "But you might get a seat on the next one if you're lucky. It leaves in about six hours."

Ryan muttered a string of swear words under his breath.

Della pasted a sweet smile on her face. "There's nothing else for it. You'll have to get this plane, Ryan," she said calmly. "Your sister will be expecting you."

Ryan shot her a quelling glance, but before he could raise any objections, Della said quickly, "I'll catch the next plane."

A short time later, Della grinned as she watched Ryan's plane take off from the runway. She took her mobile phone from her bag and tapped in a number.

"Your husband? He has gone?" The voice had a thick French accent which sent a delicious tingle down Della's spine.

"He's on his way to Ireland for his sister's wedding."

"The Paris plane is on time?"

"Yes. I'll see you soon."

"You have your ticket… and everything you need?"

Della reached inside her jacket and pulled her ticket from a pocket stitched into the lining. "As if I'd forget my ticket," she laughed. Then, more seriously, she added, "I don't need anything else."

After switching off the phone, she looked at her watch. She had just enough time to apply some purple lipstick.

ABOUT THE AUTHOR

Margaret formerly worked as a newspaper journalist but now writes mostly fiction. Her short stories have appeared in magazines in the UK and Australia

When The Cat's Away

The mice play fast and loose with Harry
Truman's belongings in this intriguing crime caper

By Steve Beresford

Bernice Rhodes – Bernie to her friends – watched as Harry Truman drove away from his house.

"OK, let's go," she said.

"Give him a few minutes," said Jack Tyler, who was sitting next to her in the parked car.

"Why? He's gone." She turned to Jack. "I know he's not coming back for at least two hours." She had done her homework and knew all there was to know about Harry Truman's regular movements.

"He might come back," said Jack. "Believe me, it happens all the time. Forgot to switch on the answering machine. Left his darts behind. Wanted to do just one last check on the dog."

"Truman doesn't have a dog," Bernie said impatiently.

"I'm just saying there are a hundred different reasons why people return home immediately."

"You're the expert," she finally conceded with a sigh.

Jack Tyler had a shady past and a rap sheet longer than his arm – which only added to his attraction. If anyone knew the finer points of breaking and entering, he did.

So they waited. Fifteen minutes in all. Bernie got restless, but Jack stayed calm, as always. For him it was just another job. Bernie, however, had unfinished business with Harry Truman.

She had a point to prove.

"Now we can go," Jack said finally. "And remember, act cool. Look confident and no one bats an eyelid at anything."

They got out of the car and crossed the road. Bernie carried a briefcase. Jack had all his tools crammed in the pockets of his smart suit. They could have passed for two double-glazing sales people. Market researchers doing

Crime Caper

She'd stepped over the line

Bernie had unfinished business with Harry Truman. She had a point to prove

a survey. Jehovah's Witnesses.

Even so, walking up to Truman's house, Bernie felt very exposed. It was mid-afternoon, after all. But Jack had assured her daytime was the best time for burglary.

"No alarm," she said, nodding up at the front façade.

"That's how I like it." He grinned. "And you'd better knock," he added. "Just in case someone's in that you don't know about."

Bernie knocked. Knocked again. Knocked a third time. No one answered. Jack had slipped round the back after the second knock. Bernie checked her surroundings. She was now hidden on all sides by the tall hedges of Truman's front garden. She followed Jack via the unlocked side gate.

He was fiddling with the lock on the kitchen door. Two panes of **Continued overleaf...**

ILLUSTRATION: ISTOCKPHOTO

Crime Caper

Continued from previous page
glass were already lying on the grass, taped up and removed from the doorframe. He explained how they had given him access to the bolts at top and bottom. He hadn't found a key though, so he was picking the mechanism.

The tumblers clicked. He stowed his tools, turned the handle and strode in through the open door.

Bernie knew that as soon as she

of it all made it so, so right.

Jack checked his watch.

"Time to get going," he said. "Will you be all right?"

"I'll be fine," she told him. She ushered him through the house to the unlocked kitchen door. "And I'll see you later. Afterwards."

She watched him go, knowing she couldn't have done this without him. As a reformed burglar he made the perfect partner for this job.

She was breathless and tingling. The wrongness of it all made it so, so right

entered she would be breaking the law, but then she thought of Harry Truman – and she stepped across the threshold anyway.

A rush of adrenaline heightened her senses. Her skin prickled but she had work to do. She followed Jack through the house, hunting and gathering. Each valuable item was deposited in the lounge until a huge pile sat on and around the coffee table. CDs and DVDs. Silverware and jewellery. A camera. His passport.

Bernie had to admit she felt more alive than she had for a long, long time. The experience was almost dizzying in its intensity.

"Fun, isn't it?" Jack caught her eye and grinned at her.

"It's amazing," she whispered. Bernie was breathless and tingling with excitement. The wrongness

Then she returned inside to wait for Harry Truman to return. All his valuable belongings lay scattered around her in disarray. He had rebuffed her approaches once, twice and then a third time.

Now she had a point to prove.

Bernice Rhodes – ruthless burglar alarm saleswoman – would show Harry Truman just how vulnerable his house was. If this demonstration didn't clinch a sale, nothing would…

ABOUT THE AUTHOR

As well as a talented writer, Steve Beresford is an avid reader. "My very favourite places are bookshops," he tells us. "I sometimes even have dreams about them!"

Within These Walls

There's so much to take in on the tour round the historic castle – so many loves and lives, begun and ended…

Who is following the tour guide?

By Elizabeth Binns

The tour guide was a lady of uncertain age with rosy cheeks and the air of the over-enthusiastic amateur. From her sensible shoes right up to her old felt hat, perched at a peculiarly jaunty angle, she exuded a love of her task that went way beyond this being a "little thing she did to keep active" every Tuesday and Thursday.

She welcomed everyone to the castle and began her standard talk in a prim, twittering soprano. Although it was clearly the same commentary that she gave several times a day, she retained a breathy excitement in her voice.

The visitors were invited to follow her through the gatehouse, and imagine how it must have felt to arrive on horseback in the fourteenth century.

As the group trailed behind this wandering mine of information, they began to form distinct elements. There were those who could imagine every room as it was in its heyday, those who waited like circling vultures for the poor lady to make a historical slip, children who just wanted to run off and play Robin Hood on the battlements, and a rather deaf old lady who kept on commenting that everything could do with a good dust.

Crossing the bailey, the tour guide made a sweeping waving gesture and proudly announced that the varied architectural styles of this most photogenic castle had led to it "starring" in several television dramas, from Shakespeare to Sir Walter Scott and Jane Austen. It had even, and here the lips pursed and she sounded as if it were not the highest honour it could receive, appeared in an episode of *Dr Who*. Several small boys immediately stopped hunting Sir Guy of Gisborne and now turned corners in the heart-stopping expectation of Cybermen.

In a far more enthusiastic tone, the guide told the group how Rebecca had threatened to throw herself off the East Tower, Mr Knightley had proposed in the rose garden, Malvolio had been kept in the stables and, oh, Miss Marple had found a body in the library!

Next, the party continued through the Great Hall, where only the night before Ye Olde Mediaeval Banquet had been held. Could everyone be careful, because chicken bones among the rushes were inclined to be slippery.

Here in the chapel were the young women who died in childbirth...

The Hall was dim and cavernous and motes of dust danced like minute golden fairies in the shafts of light from the narrow windows. The later part of the building smelled of beeswax polish.

The panelled rooms were almost cosy, despite the disdainful glances from the the portraits of previous occupants. They stared from their gilded frames, frozen forever in their velvets, silks and brocades.

The tour finished in the Chapel, where the tombs and memorials told the story of the family more accurately. Here were the young women who died in childbirth; the children who never outgrew the clothes in which they were painted; the wandering son who drowned on a voyage to the Indies, and, most ostentatiously, the knights. They lay, stone or marble-faced, upon their tombs, much the same excepting their fashion of armour. Sir Hugh fought at Agincourt, Sir Thomas at Bosworth Field, Sir Geoffrey at Naseby.

The atmosphere was musty and a little chill. A voice from the back of the group asked hopefully if the castle was haunted.

The guide laughed a little self-consciously. It was a surprisingly schoolgirl giggle for a lady of her years. She really could not say, only she herself had never actually seen anything. Hopeful Voice thanked her with a sigh.

The group trickled out of the Chapel, heading for the gift shop and tea room, anticipating postcards and Eccles cakes.

Hopeful Voice walked rather dejectedly down the nave, and then stopped suddenly, mouth agape! The glowing figure of a woman in flowing dress walked silently across the nave, pausing for a moment to stare at the visitor.

The apparition raised a hand in vague greeting and smiled graciously before walking through the bell tower door, which was shut. Hopeful Voice gave a strangled gurgle and rushed out into the sunlight.

Perhaps she did not like the way I smile…

ABOUT THE AUTHOR

"My first published work was *From Trench & Turret, Royal Marines Letters and Diaries, 1914-1918.* Writing has always been important to me."

The Softest Sigh

Enjoy this tender story, told by a concerned mother whose heart may just be broken

By Hilary Halliwell

There's our Becky, all cuddled up with Scooby her much loved Heinz 57 pooch. They're snuggled together in front of the fire and both are dreaming. Scooby's little legs go ten to the dozen as he dozes and Becky smiles contentedly as she slumbers.

Tonight my heart is as warm as the glowing coals that sparkle and crack behind the old fireguard here in our unremarkable little house. My husband Tim puts his arm around me and we watch together here in the fire's glow, so grateful for this time together; our little family complete again.

Scooby drapes a paw over Becky's hand as if to keep her safe. I can hear them breathing in the quiet of the house, my little girl and her faithful dog; it doesn't get any better than this...

The summer seems a distant memory now as autumn takes hold and the evenings draw in. Morning frosts with misty nights and the scent of wood-smoke have replaced humid days and long balmy nights of summer.

But this year I'm not saddened by summer's demise, because for us the changing season has brought with it peace and happiness back into our lives.

And that's something that, for just a while, I thought would never bless us again.

As I sit silently watching them, my eyes mist and a tear of happiness trickles down my face. Tim takes my hand in his; he knows what I'm feeling, because he's feeling it too and no words are necessary. And, as I remember those dark days not so long ago, I thank everything in the universe for this simple pleasure.

The soft sigh of the machine that keeps our daughter breathing fills the room with its rhythmic sound as I stand frozen in time.

I don't know why I made her wait for a pet

Her dark relaxed eyebrows show nothing of the trauma, nor the awfulness

She looks perfect; almost like normal, except for the tubes and machines, and the doctors and the nurses that efficiently bustle in and out of this sterile room constantly monitoring her progress.

Long feathery eyelashes frame sleeping eyes of deepest conker brown. Above them, dark relaxed eyebrows show nothing of the trauma, nor the awfulness of the situation we are in now.

As I gently kiss her brow the blush of a bruise across her forehead is the only clue to what's happened. It's half hidden by her glossy dark fringe that still smells of shampoo and happiness.

I want to scoop her up in my arms like I did when she was just a baby. Then I'd carry her off to her bed and read her favourite bedtime stories about a naughty puppy called Scooby and all the mischievous scrapes he got into. **Continued overleaf...**

Continued from previous page

"Mummy, can I have another Scooby story? I'm not tired! One day I'm going to have a dog and I'll call him Scooby…" She'd yawned.

I so want to turn back the clock to make everything like it used to be just hours ago; when life was normal and my daughter ran and played like any other happy eight year old, enjoying her little red bike in the warm summer sun with not a care in the world.

I want the dreams and hopes that I had for her future restored. But all we have right now is the ghostly sigh of the machine that keeps our Becky alive and in our world. And for that, I am grateful.

When Becky was born I felt that at last, I was complete; we were complete. We'd waited seven long years, me and my Tim for our precious little girl. And when at last she did arrive, she filled our lives with happiness and a feeling of contentment.

We'd worked and saved hard; we'd built a home and had done everything in the proper order. And then, after four years of happy marriage it was time for us to have our longed for baby. Trouble is, nature has this annoying habit of not conforming to your plans. There was nothing amiss but we ended up having to wait patiently for another three long years to finally become parents.

So – you see, when at last I held our newborn daughter in my arms, that long wait made her all the more precious to us.

We didn't spoil her, well only with love and you can never have too much of that, can you? Besides, she was, she is, a lovely child. She's totally unselfish, very caring, everyone loves her, and I truly don't remember a day when she didn't cast the sun over all of us with her smile.

As she grew from baby to toddler, and then to little girl, so too her character grew and blossomed with her. She has this sunny smile that makes you forget what she's done to upset you in the first place. She can light up the room with that infectious, happy grin of hers, can our Becky.

Three weeks have gone by in a haze; three long weeks I've sat by this little bed surrounded by life saving technology, willing my precious little girl to get better.

I've told her stories, planned her

next birthday party with her while she's slept on. I've told her all about the puppy we're going to get her as soon as she's well enough, hopefully in time for her next birthday. She's always wanted a dog and now I don't know why I made her wait.

She loves animals, does Becky. She says she wants to be a veterinary nurse when she grows up. If she grows up… and now the tears spill down my cheeks at the

the ambulance had come and taken my Becky away, with its blue flashing light and noisy siren blaring. Then I saw a distraught woman standing by a red car and I heard her say to a policeman, "I just didn't see her. The bike came from nowhere…"

She's crying and I feel both angry and sorry for her at the same time. I blame her, I blame me. How could this be allowed to happen to my little girl?

She's always loved animals and we'll get her a puppy as soon as we can

realisation that, just perhaps, she may not get that chance to fulfil her dreams for the future.

We'd always encouraged her to be independent; I think it's so important for a child to be given a little freedom, even in this scary world of ours. Besides, our little cul-de-sac is safe; we hardly see a car all day and she never goes too far from the garden gate.

I'd heard the screech of brakes, a child's scream, and then people and panic. I'd felt a strange feeling in the pit of my tummy. I just knew something dreadful had happened at that moment and I was right.

I rushed outside frantically calling her name. Meg my neighbour had run towards me and held me back. She'd held me tight and had tried to calm me. And then

Meg drove me to the hospital. Silent and careful, both of us nervous, dreading what we may find when we get there.

Tim was called from work, I remember him arriving in A&E, the sight of his ashen face, the warmth of his breath on my face, wet with tears. I remember his strength as he held me tightly in his arms.

"Come on now, I'm here, I'm here, love. She needs us to be strong. We have to believe with all our hearts that she'll make it; and she will, I know she will…"

I remember the doctors talking about scans and swelling and that only time would tell. I recall that isolation room, the sigh of the respirator and Becky's face during the dark night that seemed to go **Continued overleaf…**

Continued from previous page
on and on, forever…

But hours turned into tortured days and still she slept; sometimes a little twitch or an eye movement under those luscious eyelashes of hers, or just the feeling that she could hear me and understand my soothing words as I willed her to fight for life, to survive.

I watched and Tim slept. Tim watched while I fitfully dozed. But when I managed to drift off the dreams were worse than the reality, and he'd hold me and we'd keep the vigil together, long night after long night.

We played her favourite music; traced Incey Wincey Spider on the palm of her hand just like she'd adored when she was tiny. We

without them, but then, that's what family's all about, isn't it…?

Becky is still lost in the land of dreams, we miss her and we want our baby back, oh how we want our baby back…

It's Thursday again, four weeks since that awful day when everything changed in our world. Another week has gone by in a haze of hospital activity. But today is different because there's news, there's very good news.

They tell us that the signs are good and that her level of consciousness improves with every passing day. I feel hope returning like an old friend to comfort me, and begin to believe that we may get through this.

I can hardly believe my ears as her little voice fills the room with magic

prayed hard and searched for a sign of life, a sign that our Becky was still there; there behind the almost perfect mask of her lovely calm and serene face.

The doctors and nurses can't always answer my questions because they just don't know the answers but I feel I have no option but to ask them none the less.

Our mums and dads bolster Tim and me. They share our vigils, our hopes and our moments of near despair. I don't know what we'd do

The doctors and nurses have been wonderful. Together we've bathed Becky, talked to her, massaged her little legs that are normally never still. I've regularly wet her lips with oversized pink cotton buds that taste of mint.

As we're sitting with our darling child the miracle that we've prayed for finally happens on a warm, late summer evening, just as I'm telling her all about the "get well" cards and presents from her chums that fill every space in this little room.

At first I don't believe my eyes or more importantly, my ears.

A soft little sigh, is what I hear but its not the respirator this time. The slight shift in her position folowed by the whispered words that I've longed to hear confirm my prayers have been answered…

Her little voice suddenly fills the hospital room with magic.

"I love you, Mummy and Daddy…"

And now, the room is full of gasps and sighs made, not by the machine that brought her back to us. No, these are deep sighs of relief, joy, and utter elation.

Becky opens her birthday presents with her daddy's help, while two proud grannies dab at their eyes as we all marvel at the progress she's made over the past few days. She seems almost back to normal in many ways, if a little unsteady, but we'll soon have her strong again. She's more precious and loved than ever on this her birthday. This special day that I feared may never come.

With our help and her dad's strong arms, Becky looks out of the hospital window. Both granddads are in the car park below. They hold the tiny puppy aloft for our Becky to see; the look on her face is priceless as the little golden bundle wriggles and wags his tiny tail as if on cue…

"Thanks Mummy, thanks Dad – he's so – brilliant, I'll call him Scooby!" Becky squeals with delight as her very own pet makes his debut, as promised and on time for this, the best birthday ever.

We've a way to go yet, but with physiotherapy and lots of love, I know we'll get there the three of us – oh and, Scooby of course.

The warmth from the fire can only begin to imitate the warmth I feel in my heart tonight as we sit and watch. Our little daughter is back where she belongs, and all thanks to the skills of the doctors and nurses, faith, hope and, last but not least, the softest of sighs…

ABOUT THE AUTHOR

Hilary, mother of two grown-up sons, lives with husband Mike and two cats in Dorset. Hilary says, "My inspiration comes from life and all that it brings – happy and sad."

Fancy That!

Fascinating facts that make you go "wow"!

Not A Word

The word Bible is not mentioned once in the entire works of William Shakespeare

● In golf, a birdie is one shot under par and an eagle is two shots under par.

WOW! ● The seven heavens in the Muslim religion are Silver, Gold, Pearl, White Gold, Silver & Fire, Ruby & Garnet and the Divine Light Impossible For Mortal Man To Describe.

All For Sale

Japan has one vending machine for every 23 people, selling everything from potted plants to iPods.

Fact!

Vincent van Gogh only sold one painting during his lifetime

● **The word hexadactylism means having an extra finger or toe. Having more than one extra digit is called polydactylism**

● Lady Jane Gray was Queen of England for just nine days before her execution in 1553.

● **The average "ten-gallon hat" would actually only hold six pints.**

● At 15, Baker Street station has more escalators than any other stop on the London Underground.

WOW! ● The "21-gun salute" dates from the days of sailing ships, when British navy vessels had a maximum of 21 guns along each side.

● **In Singapore, the phrase "half-past six" means "not completely sane", just as we use "All at sixes and sevens" to mean in a state of confusion.**

● According to a scientific paper published by Cambridge physicists Thomas Fink and Yong Mao, there are 85 different ways of tying a man's tie in nine movements or fewer – although they concluded that only 13 ways were practical or aesthetically pleasing.

● **The "pieces of eight" beloved of Long John Silver were Spanish dollars, which were marked with a figure 8 because there were eight reals to a dollar.**

● The largest hen's egg on record weighed 14 ounces.

Stretch Limo

The open-topped Lincoln limousine in which John F. Kennedy was shot in 1963 was still being used by President Jimmy Carter in 1977

Sir Krishna

Sir Ben Kingsley's real name is Krishna Bhanji

● Incredibly, two Barbie dolls are sold every second.

● **According to a survey, 80% of Icelanders either believe in elves or refuse to rule out their existence.**

● 46.4% of women buy new shoes or boots for special occasions.

Fact!

Donald Pleasance, Telly Savalas, Charles Gray (pictured) and Max von Sydow have all played the James Bond villain Blofeld in different films

Green Fingers Warm Hearts

How does your garden grow? You'll enjoy this engaging story of a common love of all things natural

By Anne Goring

S tanding by the window holding the letter I can see it's a wild morning. The gale turns the garden into a maelstrom of flying leaves and whipping branches.

I'm so glad I don't have to go out. I've plenty of time to think things through before I call my daughter. Oh, I know what my answer should be. Sell up. Move to Rosedale. Everybody says it's the best possible course.

Janet says confidentially she'll see to everything about the move. "You'd be foolish not to sell right now, Mother. The house is far too big for you and such a drain on your finances. Once you've sold, you'll be comfortably off. There'll be no fretting about heating bills

and council tax. Rosedale is such a happy place. Caring staff, lots of outings, no responsibilities. Just say and I'll organise it so that you don't have to worry about a thing."

Janet's very efficient. I suppose she wouldn't hold an important job in London if she wasn't. She did make the suggestion that we might both sell up and buy a bigger flat in the same complex she lives in now so she could keep an eye on me, but I know in my bones that wouldn't work. It isn't that we don't get on – we rub along comfortably on visits but Janet would never countenance a garden and I would never want to be stuck three flights up in the middle of a city, however magnificent the view. Besides, long-term living together might not work. I shouldn't like for us not to be friends because she

Janet would never ever countenance a garden and I would become resentful

And

I loved to spend
time in the garden

felt I was a burden or me to become resentful because of not liking the kind of life she enjoys.

Down at the end of the garden young Tracey's silver birch sapling bends and twists in the wind. I remember how I drove her to the garden centre and let her choose something to replace the old white lilac that had died. She took on board everything I'd told her about needing a tree with an eventual height and spread to mask the **Continued overleaf…**

telegraph pole out on the road, but not too invasive. She dithered over a rowan, but settled for the birch. I'm glad she did because with her long, skinny limbs and twiggy hair and her eyebrows and ears glinting with silver rings and studs, it's almost as if she embodies the spirit of the tree. It makes me smile every time I look at it.

It was a good summer, the summer of Tracey. At my lunch club we were told about these young people from the local school who were running a project to help out elderly people with household jobs they couldn't do.

Shopping, gardening and so on. I was in two minds. Janet of course was dead against it.

"You're far too vulnerable, Mother," she'd cried down the phone. "You've no idea what sort of yobbo you might get."

bluntly questioning everything I asked her to do, seemed far less promising. Yet the serious one hated getting her nails messed up and didn't last two visits. Tracey didn't even bat a mascara-ed eyelash at worms and slugs and was positively fascinated by the wildlife that haunted my little pond.

By summer's end Tracey knew more than I did about damsel-flies and dragonflies and pond skaters and had created special wood heaps to shelter the froglets when they made their way out of the water. She quickly picked up the names of the plants and which ones did best in shade or sunshine, which plants were weeds to be discouraged and which tiny self-sown seedlings might be left to flower for another season.

"There's a lot more to this gardening than I thought," she'd say, energetically tackling a strand

I was vulnerable and had no idea what kind of volunteer would offer to help

Perhaps that's what decided me. Janet was always so sure she was right. "They'll be supervised," I said firmly. "And the weeding always gets out of hand this time of the year."

There were two of them at first. A serious, chatty girl, who was all caring looks and willingness. Tracey, chewing gum, regarding me with sharp, feline eyes, and

of recalcitrant bindweed or carefully hoeing between the petunias and stocks and sunflowers. "Beats stacking shelves."

The school project was officially over in July and she had a holiday job at the supermarket but Tracey kept dropping in all that summer and well into the autumn term until the garden was tidied for the

winter, bulbs planted, pruning done, leaves swept up and composted. Even after that she sometimes knocked as she came home from school and joined me in a cup of tea and a browse through the new gardening catalogues. Making me laugh with her laconic comments on her schoolwork and her form mates.

But by Christmas she'd gone, along with all her raggle-taggle family, when her step-dad managed to find a job in Manchester.

I miss her regular visits, but she does keep in touch.

I don't think that they moved up-market though from what she says. It was bad enough being in that damp, uncared-for terrace down by the river here, but the council estate where she is now is pretty rough from what she lets slip. She's working full time in a supermarket now. I'm glad she got a steady job and touched that she still rings to ask about the garden and the tree.

"I'd like to plant one here," she says, "but my brothers say they won't have room for the old cars they do up if I start messing about with the tiny bit of garden we've got." She's always full of questions. Are the bulbs up? Did you get a lot of frog spawn in the pond this year? How's the veggie patch?

I had to tell her last spring that I'd decided – well, Janet had – to grass over the vegetable patch. That was after I'd caught a nasty flu bug and ended up for two weeks in hospital with pneumonia. I was still feeling pretty washed out when Janet started on at me to forget all about the garden and sell up.

"Really, Mother, you know it's all too much for you."

"I'll be right as ninepence when the weather improves."

"Well at least forget about planting vegetables. It's ridiculous to put yourself to all that trouble when you give most of them away."

"But I enjoy –"

"I know, dear. But you must be sensible. At your age you should be thinking of putting your feet up and having a good rest, not wearing yourself out."

"Better to wear out than rust away," I muttered, but I felt too weary at the time to put up much of an argument. She had men round quick as a flash clearing everything out and laying turf. And **Continued overleaf…**

got them to come back every other week this last summer and cut the grass. Once I got my strength back though, I dug out a patch at the back where she hardly ever goes and planted lettuce and beetroot and radishes. I hate not having a bit of salad stuff to pull. I've got cabbage and winter cauliflower in there now. Janet didn't half look black when she sneaked up there the other day and found out.

"You're incorrigible, Mother," she said, a bit tight-lipped. "You worry me, you really do. How do you think I'd feel if you strained yourself or fell or something?"

And how do you think I'd feel if I couldn't spend a bit of each day fiddling in my garden, was what I wanted to say but didn't.

"Upset, I know, love," was all I said. "I'm sorry. It's just that it's not work to me, it's pleasure."

"Well, once you're in Rosedale," she said in an encouraging voice, "you'll soon learn to relax and take enjoyment from sitting in their pretty garden and not having the stress of caring for it. Oh, and by the way dear, I know someone who'd like to buy the car. He collects Morris Minors. He doesn't mind a bit that it's acquired a few bumps and scratches."

"Only a couple," I protested. "And one wasn't my fault. Someone banged the door in the precinct car park. Besides, I'm not

thinking of giving up driving yet and I don't go very far. Just up to the shops and the lunch club and perhaps the garden centre."

"You did catch the bumper a real whack on the gatepost, last month," Janet said firmly. "I don't want to think of you having a more serious accident. Besides, you won't need the car in Rosedale."

Sad, but we don't really communicate, me and Janet. Not on a level that matters. We never have done unfortunately.

The wind whirls the leaves in a gold and russet eddy over the scarlet geraniums that by now I should have potted up and put in the conservatory for the winter. The mild weather's kept them going, but with this Rosedale business hanging over me I haven't had the heart to start on the autumn jobs.

I sigh. Can't put it off any longer. I move to the phone and dial

Janet's number. She doesn't really like me phoning her at the office, but this is so important to me that I want to get it over with quickly.

"Mother? What is it?" I hear the hint of panic in her voice before it turns to astonishment, then crossness. "You can't mean this… It's quite ridiculous. Look, please don't do anything in a hurry. I haven't time to discuss this now.

centre where we bought the silver birch and she's planning to go to the local college to study horticulture. We had a long chat on the phone last night and talked about her options.

"If you're absolutely sure," she said, quite shyly for her. "I can be a pig to live with. But if you could put up with me as a lodger… well, that'd be great."

I feel like trees must do in springtime, full of a joyful sense of new purpose

I'll come round… Not tonight. I've got a meeting. Tomorrow."

"There's no need," I say calmly. "I want you to know that I'm truly thankful for everything you do for me, but I'm not in my dotage yet, love. Perhaps there'll come a time for Rosedale, but not this year."

"You're being taken advantage of!" she says, but I know she's wrong. She might be a whizz at her important job but she's a bit blinkered in some ways is Janet.

I can bring the geraniums in now, I think with relief, as I put the phone down. Perhaps the trees in spring feel like I do now. Full of a joyful sense of purpose and anticipation for the new season.

I re-read Tracey's letter. She hates Manchester and she's working out her notice at the supermarket. She's got an interview for a job at the garden

"It's not out of charity," I said with mock sternness. "You'll pay your way and give me a hand in the garden. And I may make you drive me to the shops in the Morris from time to time."

"Phew, that's a relief," she said. "I thought you were going to make me do the washing up."

We laughed together at that. I don't think Tracey'll ever make a domestic goddess.

"So how's my silver birch?"

"Doing well," I said. "Just like us."

The boutique had perfectly pretty lingerie in every colour

By Pamela Pickton

D orothy stood for a moment looking at the present. The shimmer of silky pale green with a glimpse of lace peeping out, still half hidden by the tissue paper. She had crumpled the present up and tossed it on to the kitchen

worktop amidst the coffee cups, all the relics of her sister's flying visit. Dorothy's birthday visit fitted into Yvonne's lunch hour; the pretty panties bought no doubt in the shop near where Yvonne worked, wrapped up hastily on the way.

They were so pretty, Dorothy thought, taking them out of the paper and draping them across the

ounter

out in this fun story!

taps while she washed up the coffee things. If only they would fit her, and if only they didn't say *Tuesday*. On the front of the briefs was a little white lacy heart, enclosing the embroidered weekday. Today was Tuesday, maybe that was why Yvonne had chosen that pair. All ready for a special birthday treat.

Dorothy pulled out the ironing board and the basket full of crumpled clothes and plugged in the iron. She spread the briefs out on the work surface in front of her so that she could admire them while she worked.

Tuesday was never their day. Phil was always too tired, so there wouldn't be much point in stepping into the frillies when he got home. Tuesday was his late night, anyway. In fact, there were more and more late work nights these days. That was the trouble…

Saturday had always been the best time – soon becoming the only time. And lately, Phil had on many weekends been forced to work away from home. Dorothy knew it couldn't be helped, he was trying to build up his business. Phil hadn't seemed to be missing anything. He was so preoccupied with work worries, he probably didn't even remember.

Dorothy picked up the panties, stretching out the elastic with her fingers and holding them flat against her sensible jeans. Somehow, all glamour had gone, once the honeymoon nighties had worn out. Getting out of bed in the night to crying babies called for warm winceyette with long sleeves. Blow that wretched Tuesday! Yvonne had probably picked up a pair without even **Continued overleaf…**

Continued from previous page

looking, just because she had a boyfriend for every night of the week. Every day was lucky for her.

Dorothy unplugged the iron and stuffed all the un-ironed things back in the cupboard. She pulled on her jacket, picked up her keys and treated the clock to an accusing glare as she ran out the door. She had to pick up the children, give them tea and then rush them to Brownies. Tuesday was a tiring evening for her, too, but if she hurried she would make it.

At the little lingerie shop – around the corner from Yvonne's work, right enough – the briefs were festooned on a pole, hanging just like blossoms on a tree, Dorothy thought. Green and lilac, white and pink. Around the pole was a counter piled with more pants, all jumbled up as though everyone had been hunting for their favourite day of the week.

not change her expression when Dorothy politely enquired about Saturday pants, but long-sufferingly bent to a cupboard beneath the counter. Dorothy wondered if she would dare do as much as blink if she whispered, *"You see, we only do it on Saturday…"* The assistant turned and faced Dorothy accusingly.

"We only have one 'Saturday' left madam. Pink."

Well, one pink Saturday is exactly what I need, thought Dorothy, handing over the green ones. "Pink, pink to make the boys wink" she sang in time with her footsteps as she hurried out to meet the girls.

Later, Phil switched his eyes from his bedtime book to his undressing wife.

"Saturday?" he enquired, a confused expession on his face.

"Yes!" Dorothy sat decisively on

The briefs were festooned on a pole, hanging just like blossoms on a tree

And the more frenziedly she searched, the more it dawned on Dorothy why Yvonne had picked Tuesday – all the panties left were all weekdays, and most Tuesday. *It must be everybody's late work night*, she laughed.

The poker-faced assistant did

the edge of the bed and took the book away. "Why not?"

Lying peacefully together afterwards, Phil said, "I always thought you were too tired on Tuesday night."

"What?" Dorothy suddenly shot up from the pillow and stared

down at him unbelieving.

"Well, you're usually tired during the week. If it's not the Brownies, it's the kids' tea or the weekly shop or the washing machine breaking down and leaking again…"

"Oh Phil," she laughed, brushing the hair from his forehead. "You don't mean… I mean, I thought…"

He kissed her. "You surely didn't think that I could ever be too tired to notice you, did you?"

And later again, Dorothy sighed, "Oh, what a pity that tomorrow's Wednesday, then Thursday, then Friday. Then I suppose you're away for the weekend again?"

"Only one more trip and I think we'll be seeing the light."

"Oh, darling," she hugged him. "Do you mean weekends again? Taking the kids out, going out to dinner, having our own special evenings together?"

"Ssh!" he took her hand. "I'll tell you what…" he sat up on his elbow and looked down at her. "Wear those panties every night."

"But they say, 'Saturday.'"

"I won't tell anybody if you won't," he laughed.

"And anyway, why shouldn't it be Saturday night every night?"

By Eleanor Sayer

A Fine

Women long for romance and men long for lasagne – but they can still make each other happy

Kate tumbled through the lift doors, a whirlwind of cold, wet material. Umbrella, raincoat, bag; sodden from the downpour outside. Droplets of freezing water scattered freely over everything as she struggled to straighten herself up.

"You're late, Kate," warned Anna gently as she passed the mirrored pillar in which Kate was looking, desperately trying to make herself look a bit more presentable.

"I know… please tell me Stan isn't ready to start the morning meeting yet?" she said.

"Not yet but you'd better hurry, he will be any minute."

Kate glanced at herself one final time. Her hair was flattened to her scalp with the rain, but she liked to think she could pass it off as a sleek, corporate style. The raincoat had caught the worst of the stormy weather, and her suit, though rumpled from the commute, was just about passable.

She nodded at herself. Ready to face the day.

"Morning, Kate. Oh no, what happened to you? You look absolutely drenched! Did you get caught in the rain? I would have done, but Toby absolutely insisted he drive me to work in his Porsche. He's taking me to Barcelona this weekend, you see, and we can't run the risk of a red nose, can we?"

Claudia, 5' 9" of perfection, the bane of Kate's office life.

"Morning Claudia. I thought it was Prague this weekend?" Kate asked through gritted teeth.

"Oh no, Prague was the weekend just gone! Do keep up, Kate! Sounds like Dan needs to take you away for the weekend, treat you to some R&R!" Claudia laughed her trilling little laugh and walked away. Kate sighed. It was going to be one of those days.

Trudging through the commuter-jammed streets of the city that evening, Kate recalled Claudia's words.

Dan did need to take her away… or take her out… or even just get a takeaway. Kate frowned. Dan did love her, she knew that, but since they'd moved in together a year ago, things had changed. Dan had never been one for big romantic gestures, but they had enjoyed a good night out together as much as any other couple.

But somehow all that had been

Romance

Where had the
romance gone?

Dan did love her but he had never really been one for over-the-top gestures

put on the back burner. Life was still good, but the spontaneity of those early days seemed to have gone and she missed it.

Kate walked faster, indignation rising. Was she no longer worth the effort? Toby lived in a different part of town to Claudia, but that didn't stop him driving her to work when it was raining, or sending bunches of flowers to the office, or forever carting her off on romantic weekend breaks.

The closest Dan got to giving her a break was when he abandoned her for four hours every Saturday morning to play football with his mates.

By the time Kate let herself in
Continued overleaf…

Continued from previous page

the front door, she was itching for an argument. A message on the answering machine from Dan informed her he was working late, which fuelled her irritation further. *I'll just cook dinner and wash up too, then, shall I?* she thought, with a touch of belligerence.

Dinner was very therapeutic. She crashed dishes and clanged pots together, muttering at the onions like they were her worst enemy. By the time the bolognese was ready, Kate felt far more mellow, though she still felt unsure about Dan.

In the weeks that followed, Claudia seemed to have a new "Toby" story every day. By comparison, Kate's steady life with Dan seemed dull.

Dan was to be away on business for a week, leaving on a night flight, so Kate prepared a meal for the evening of his departure.

"Good lasagne, love." Dan stood up and stretched. Bending down, he kissed her briefly on the mouth. "Running late, see you next week." He moved towards the hallway to grab his cases.

It was the last straw.

"Is that all I get?" Kate thundered.

Dan stopped, startled by the outburst. "What do you mean?"

"I mean, where has all the romance gone?" Kate snapped. "We never go away for the weekend, you never send me to a spa, we rarely go out. All you do is

work and play football on Saturdays. And when have you made me a lasagne? Am I not worth the effort?"

Dan stood, completely taken aback by her tirade.

Belatedly, Kate wondered if she had gone too far. She tried to backtrack. "It's just, you never send flowers, or buy me chocolates, or… or…" she faltered, seeing the hurt in Dan's eyes.

"Go on," he said wearily. "What else don't I do?"

She was silent, biting her lip.

He sighed, and slumped onto the sofa with a resigned air.

"I don't buy you chocolate because you say you need to lose weight. Flowers just die. I play football to try to keep in shape so you still fancy me. You get bored watching a film so how you would cope doing nothing at a spa for two days I have no idea, and we never go out because I'm working hard to save money for…" He broke off.

"For what?" Kate asked hesitantly in a small voice.

"For our future, assuming we have one," Dan muttered.

"Dan, I –" She broke off.

He stood up, interrupting her.

"Look, Kate, I've got to go. Maybe we shouldn't phone each other this week, I'll be working and you obviously have a lot to think about. I'll see you next Saturday."

On Tuesday, Kate was called into Stan's office.

"I just wanted to tell you, Kate, that the input you had in the Collins case has been noticed. We're very pleased with your contribution and feel you have the potential to go far in the company. In fact, there's a position for account supervisor coming up in a few weeks, and I think you should

She crashed dishes and muttered at the onions like they were her worst enemy

Kate nodded miserably.

He gave her a quick kiss on the cheek. "Bye," he said softly, and then he was gone.

Kate stayed on the sofa for a long time after Dan left. She already regretted her words; the sentiment behind them was beginning to sound rather whiney, even to her ears. It was a Saturday night, but she didn't feel any desire to be out partying. She would be happy just to curl up with a good book... and with Dan.

On Sunday morning Kate woke up to the feeling something was missing. Not just Dan, she realised, but no smell of coffee brewing, no flaky croissants on the kitchen table. The Sunday paper wasn't lying rumpled on his side of the bed. If she wanted to read it, she'd have to get it herself.

apply. You stand a very good chance of landing the job."

Kate was thrilled. She skipped out of the office that evening. She couldn't wait to tell Dan; he always was so supportive. But as she opened the door to the silent house, she remembered their row. She wished he was home, unromantic but all hers.

At the office on Friday, Kate noticed an odd vibe as soon as she walked in. Passing Claudia's desk, she opened her mouth to ask what was going on, but one look at Claudia's face, and Kate had a sinking feeling she knew.

"Hi, Claudia. How are you?" Kate faltered, unable to tear her gaze from the other woman's puffy, red-ringed eyes. Claudia opened her mouth to speak, shut it again and promptly burst into tears, **Continued overleaf...**

shooting from her desk and streaking to the Ladies.

As soon as she was out of sight, Maryanne, at the next desk, spun round, eager to fill Kate in.

"It's over," she explained breathlessly. "Turns out Claudia isn't the only girl Toby's been whisking away on romantic weekends. The flowers and gifts were to cover for times he broke their dates. When he sent her to those spas, it was so he was free to take someone else away! God knows where he gets the stamina from – he can't have spent a weekend in England since 2001!

"Claudia's devastated, especially having gone on about him like that – well, I'm just thankful my Steve wouldn't know how to organise his way out of a plastic bag!"

Kate made her way to her desk. Poor Claudia. They may not be friends (in fact Claudia irritated her to the point of insanity) but Kate could only imagine what the other woman must be feeling. Thank heaven for Dan. She mentally hugged herself at the thought of wonderful, un-flashy, steady Dan. No surprises. She grinned. That was fine by her!

That evening, as Kate opened the front door, wonderful cooking smells wafted out towards her from the kitchen and low music could be heard from the stereo.

Dan was home early! As she began to take off her coat, he appeared in the doorway from the kitchen. He looked wonderful, his brown hair tousled, as it tended to be when he was nervous or worried. He grinned when he saw her.

Kate flew across the hall into his outstretched arms.

"I missed you," she said, squeezing him tight, relishing the solid feel of him in her arms.

"I missed you, too," he whispered softly into her ear.

She leaned back, happy just to be this close to him again.

Dan, however, took a step back. "Er, dinner's almost ready," he

A week apart, and she couldn't even get him to choose *her* over dinner?

said, unhooking her hands from behind his neck.

Kate couldn't believe it. A week apart, and she couldn't even get him to choose *her* over dinner? Had their relationship really become that stale? She looked into his face and realised he looked uncomfortable. Nervous even. She felt sick. What was he worried about? Oh God, had he been cheating, too?

"What's wrong?" she asked in a

hoarse, panicky voice.

He saw her stricken expression and gave her a quick hug.

"Nothing, I just wanted to cook for you, and I don't want it to burn."

Kate could see tension lingering around the corners of his mouth, and the penny dropped. He must still be thinking about the fight they had before he went away. He had listened to what she said and was trying to make a romantic gesture. She planted a quick kiss on his cheek.

"Thanks, Dan," she said quietly.

He looked relieved. "Sit yourself down then, the wine's poured."

In the lounge, the table had been set for two, with candles, flowers, the lot. No surprises, huh? Dan came in from the kitchen, and placed a large dish on the table in front of her. Kate's gaze remained on him. He looked so handsome in the candlelight.

"Well?" Dan asked, his face anxious. Poor love, he really wants me to like his cooking, Kate thought. "It smells great," she reassured him, then looked down at the dish set in front of her.

He had made her lasagne. A huge dish of it, creamy and piping hot, cooked to perfection. And on the top, carefully written out in bright cherry tomatoes, were the words *Marry Me*.

Kate gasped and tears filled her eyes. She looked at Dan, who had quickly moved from his chair to kneel next to hers.

"I love you, Kate," he said. "I know I'm rubbish at all that romance stuff, but if you'll give me the chance I'll get better, I promise. I can change."

Kate shook her head. "Don't," she croaked. "Don't you dare! If you change one single thing, the wedding's off'."

Dan grinned, tension finally falling from his face.

"Thank God!" He laughed. "I was so nervous I had completely lost my appetite!"

Kate laughed. "And that, my love, would really be the biggest surprise of all!"

ABOUT THE AUTHOR

Eleanor lives in North Wales and works at a holiday cottage agency, which provides ample scope to daydream about beautiful UK settings for her stories

Her memory
of him was
so clear

Moonlight
Serenade

**Your heart will go
out to Nancy, still
waiting for her
handsome soldier
to return amid
the 1945
New Year
festivities**

By Patti Hales

T he gale force winds which had whipped the sea into an aggressive frenzy for the past week had finally blown themselves out. The last day of nineteen forty-five sparkled in a calm and peaceful frosty brightness. An air of expectancy and hope hung over the small community.

Inside the Stewart house, all the carpets, having been thoroughly beaten over the clothes-line, sat on freshly-polished lino; the furniture was buffed to a high gloss, and good smells were wafting through from the small kitchenette.

Bob had brought in enough coal and logs from the outside cellar to last for a couple of days and now was snoozing in his armchair, having declared that he needed to reserve what strength he had left for the festivities ahead.

"Believe me," he'd declared before drifting off, "this will be a night to remember. All the troubles are over and we've been lucky enough to come through everything as a family.

"Of course," he'd finished, his heavy eyelids fluttering, "we'll have to spare a bit of time to think of others less fortunate. Hmm?"

Stooping to close the oven door, the hostess of one of tonight's big parties, Jean, heard herself agreeing. Her response had been greeted by a soft snore.

Smiling as she straightened, she looked fondly at her husband.

Bob had been too old to go to war and for that she'd been grateful. He'd been her rock, always somehow finding the right cheering words to say to her as they'd worked side by side in his small engineering factory.

As for the younger members of the family – her years of prayers, as she'd worried and waited, had all been answered.

Their older son, Robert, was already back home with his wife, Moira, and the younger, Johnnie – Jean had had an enthusiastic letter from him only that morning – would soon be back from his long stint in the Far East.

Besides that, their four nephews – two of hers, two of Bob's – had survived the war too.

Yes, they'd all come through the years of hardship intact.

Then, wiping her hands on a cloth, she spotted the agonised expression on Nancy's pretty face

Jean's prayers had been answered; one son was home and the other on his way

ILLUSTRATION: MIKE HESLOP

Continued overleaf…

as the girl fiddled with the coloured beads edging the crocheted mat which covered the blue-striped milk jug.

Nancy seemed to be counting: red, blue, green, yellow; over and over again. Jean gnawed on her lower lip. It was physically painful to watch those slender fingers curling into tense white fists; to see her sad hazel eyes that had once been clear and filled with love and hope. Even Nancy's long chestnut hair seemed to have lost most of its former lustre.

Casualties of war, Jean decided, came in all shapes and forms. She couldn't help but wonder if the ones like her only daughter, who were still waiting for so many questions to be answered, perhaps suffered the most?

Jean wished again that she knew how to handle the dilemma. She wanted to find the right words that would take the raw edges off a

hear. The best she'd been able to offer in the end had been lots of hugs and a shoulder to cry on.

She made a mental note to herself to do everything in her power to ensure that Nancy's hurt would only be a temporary thing and that the memory of Steve, while it would never completely fade, would eventually become something to look back on with the wisdom of age and experience.

But achieving that would take a very long time. A rocky and uncertain road lay ahead – she and Bob both knew that.

Through all of this, Nancy had seemed capable of voicing only the same sequence of sentences. Very softly, but with a voice filled with determination.

"It's not one of 'those things'. Steve loves me. There has to be a reason that he hasn't come back yet. But he will. I know it."

Each time she said it, the words shot a dart into Jean's heart.

"Steve loves me. There has to be a reason why he hasn't come back yet"

kind of pain she felt she could almost reach out and touch.

She didn't want to spell out the hard facts of war-time romances – how in the heat of the moment false promises were made – because that was the last thing a tortured young woman needed to

Both she and Bob had liked the young American and had been hurt and upset at his behaviour. But they knew, too, that there didn't have to be any reason, at least not of the kind Nancy was likely to be imagining.

No, it was just the age-old story.

Steve had been suddenly recalled to the United States and he had probably, and quite under-standably, slipped back into his old life, surrounded by everything that was familiar. And his own family, thrilled to have their precious son safely home again, had most likely talked him into staying.

Added to that, there was no doubt a high school sweetheart waiting in the wings, ready to pick up the post-war reins.

Painful though it was to accept, Jean conceded to herself that, in Steve's mother's position, she might have done exactly the same thing herself.

Of course she hadn't actually said so, not in so many words… well, except to Bob, who had merely nodded sadly.

"We'll see her through it," he had said gruffly. "Somehow."

So far though, it had been an uphill battle.

Nearly at the end of her tether, Jean had roped in a couple of Nancy's close friends for assistance. In fact, it had been they who had finally persuaded the girl into going to tonight's Hogmanay Dance at the Pavilion.

"It'll be great," Beryl had declared. "Extra special. They've got the old coloured fountain working again and a terrific band.

"I know you might not think it now, but you'll enjoy it when you get there. You will, Nancy!"

There had been a long silence, then, "I don't really think so. I haven't been out for ages. Everyone must have forgotten me by now. I'll be a . . . wallflower." Nancy had responded flatly, her expression blank, yet at the same time holding a hundred memories.

Beryl's dancing blue eyes had widened. "What? You? Don't be daft! There'll be a queue forming!"

Then Maggie, seeing the small smile which had lifted the corners of her friend's full mouth, had quickly put in her twopennyworth.

"Nancy, I know you don't feel

Continued overleaf…

Continued from previous page

that you're in the mood for company, but where are you going to find peace and quiet tonight? The coal cellar?"

Good point, Jean had thought, watching from the kitchenette doorway. The whole town would be buzzing. Then Nancy had come up with another excuse.

"But I don't have anything decent to wear for a night out."

It had taken Jean no time at all to dash upstairs to the big chest on the landing.

"I think we could do something with this," she'd said on her return.

Beryl and Maggie had oohed and aahed over the shimmering blue-green sateen. Nancy had barely given it a second glance.

But again, Jean's persistence had paid off, and now she suddenly remembered that there was still the hem to be taken up.

Kneeling on the fireside rug, her mouth full of pins, she mumbled through her firmly clenched teeth.

"Round a wee bit, dear. Oh, yes, that's fine. Now a bit more… more… no, stop right there." Resting back on her heels, she cast an expert eye over the hemline. "OK," she nodded, "you can slip it off now, sweetheart."

Wordlessly, Nancy obeyed. Her mother glanced briskly at the clock on the mantelpiece.

"It's about time you were getting your hair washed. You know how

long it takes to dry. And you'll want to make it look extra nice for tonight, won't you?"

Nancy didn't appear to have heard. Still seemingly preoccupied, she wandered over to the wireless and turned the knob.

There was a hiss and a crackle, followed by a lengthy silence, then music filled the cosy room. Bob stirred momentarily and shifted position, but Jean reckoned it would be a while before he was fully awake.

She glanced anxiously at her daughter, who was propped against the wall.

Her jaw dropped. Nancy was

smiling, properly for the first time in ages. Her eyes were misty with a faraway look.

"Moonlight becomes you, it goes with your hair," Nancy sang along softly with the crooning voice, but before Jean had a chance to collect her muddled thoughts the wireless was switched off again and Nancy was heading for the door.

"Thanks, Mum, for everything," she said over her shoulder.

When she'd gone, Bob opened one eye. "What was that all about then?"

Jean could only shake her head.

B eryl was wearing a soft blue crêpe which exactly matched her eyes. Her dark blonde hair was styled into a perfect page-boy.

The soft floral fabric of Maggie's dress hugged her curvy figure; she that her gorgeous chestnut mane, rolled back from her forehead to reveal her perfect heart-shaped face, tumbled over her shoulders in a waterfall of loose curls. It was something else; a factor they couldn't quite put their finger on. But somewhere along the line, they both agreed, a minor miracle seemed to have occurred.

Nancy looked radiant, simply filled with happiness.

"Wallflower!" Beryl muttered. She raised her eyes comically as the trio headed for the bar to accept their complimentary glass of punch, courtesy of the management.

The drink was an odd shade – a sort of vivid yellowy-green.

"Best not even to question what might be in this," Maggie said in a hushed voice. "Probably –" All three of them came out with the

Her daughter was smiling for the first time in ages, a faraway look in her eyes

too had opted for the sleek, glamorous hair look.

But both girls were aware that all eyes were on Nancy. Expecting the worst – that Nancy wouldn't have made much of an effort – they'd been stunned when she'd taken off her plain beige coat.

The fact that she shimmered had nothing to do with the glossy fabric of her close-fitting dress or the fact same giggled words at exactly the same time: "Dried egg!"

They were still laughing as the band struck up.

Nancy was so glad it was the lively *In The Mood* – not one of the dreamy romantic ones – that she instantly accepted the offer to dance from John McLeod, who'd been in her class at school.
Continued overleaf…

Continued from previous page

He looked older, sadder and so thin, she thought, in his over-large brown demob suit. His too-short haircut didn't help either. It made his ears look enormous and bits of pink scalp showed through the wispy dark strands.

In spite of telling herself that it wasn't fair, she couldn't help but

"She's fallen for a Yank. Gone over there to marry him. In Idaho, wherever that might be!

"Ruddy Americans. These things never work out. Mark my words, she'll be back – with her tail between her legs and probably a couple of little ones in tow. And Yours Truly won't be there this time to pick up the pieces!"

"Ruddy Americans. These things never work out. She'll be back, mark my words"

compare him with broad-shouldered, muscular Steve whose uniforms and casual wear both looked elegant and well-tailored.

Her heart rate quickened as a clear image of his handsome face, topped by a thick thatch of dark brown hair, filled her line of vision.

John's voice, as he whirled her around the slippery floor, brought her back to reality.

"How have you been?" he asked.

"Fine," Nancy fibbed. "And you?"

John's expression reminded her of a whipped puppy. "So-so. I suppose you heard that Catherine dumped me six months ago." Nancy hadn't, but she made what she hoped were appropriate soothing noises.

"Naturally she sent me a 'Dear John' letter," he went on, his voice tinged with ironic disdain. "What else?" Then the tone changed and he became filled with a quiet fury.

Nancy suspected he would be. If it happened. Love was like that. But she merely nodded, not trusting herself to speak.

If she did, she'd have to tell him that he was wrong. That sometimes *these things*, as he'd referred to them, did work out.

When the dance finished, she made her excuses.

"Got to go and powder my nose," she said, turning quickly and pushing her way through the ever-increasing crowds.

The foyer was practically deserted. The overhead lights had been turned down, showing the colourful fountain in all its changing glory: red, blue, green, yellow, again and again.

Nancy had instinctively known it would be that way. Quite why, she wasn't sure, but her mind was filled with other things, so she chose not to dwell on the matter.

She watched the repetitive sequence for a long time, becoming lost in the soothing rhythm of the tumbling water . . .

She jumped as a hand touched her shoulder. It was Beryl. Her cheeks were bright pink.

"Quick. Quick!" she said, grabbing Nancy's arm and pulling her back towards the dancehall.

Nancy asked, "Where's the fire?" but her words were lost against the voices joining in *The White Cliffs Of Dover* with great gusto.

As they neared the back of the hall, she could see Maggie standing on tiptoe, her dark gaze searching the large ballroom. And

the expression of relief when she spotted her prey.

She waved frantically. Beryl waved back.

"Over here," Maggie mouthed.

"Over there," Beryl pointed.

"OK," Nancy said, apologising as, in the crush, she trod on someone's foot. "But I wish someone would tell me what's going on!"

Beryl opened her mouth, but no sound came out. She pointed again. This time, Nancy's eyes followed the direction of the wavering finger.

All she could see were countless backs. What, she wondered, was she supposed to be looking at?

Then as the tall man in the dark suit turned to face them, her breath caught in the back of her suddenly dry throat. The crowd seemed to melt away and seconds later she was gazing straight into his clear green eyes.

The dark hair was longer than it had been when she'd last seen him and there was a long scar puckering the tanned left cheek.

He was thinner too, and, as he moved towards her, there was no disguising Steve's limp.

But none of that mattered. Only the taste of his lips on hers, the familiar smell and touch of him as his arms closed round her.

Nancy's head spun deliciously.

He'd said he'd come back, and **Continued overleaf…**

Continued from previous page
that something inside her would let her know that he was on his way. She'd had the sign, but had been prepared for a further wait. She hadn't for a moment dared to dream that he'd return on this most special of nights.

Coming here had been merely to satisfy her anxious mum and dad.

come in person than to write to you . Also, I didn't want you to imagine the worst . . ."

Nancy, clinging tightly to him, winced as he spoke.

She had imagined the worst but, not wanting to worry them, had tried to hide this from her parents. She hoped she'd succeeded in doing exactly that.

"You said there would be some sign that you were on your way"

"I love you," Steve murmured, looking right at her.

"I love you, too," Nancy said huskily, then she narrowed her eyes. "You look as if you've been in the wars!"

A flush swept across Steve's face. His hand went up to touch the puckered scar.

"It's crazy! All these years I flew planes in and out of hellish places. Moonlight raids. And each time I came back without even a scratch." He grinned wryly. "I guess what it boils down to is that I'm a good pilot, but lousy when it comes to automobiles!"

He went on to describe the car accident. Both arms had been fractured along with his left leg. He'd been unconscious for weeks.

"That's why no-one was able to let you know, honey. Then, when the medics decided I'd live, I reckoned it would be quicker to

"I knew you'd come when you could," she said softly. "You always said I'd know when you were on your way, that there would be some kind of sign. It came this afternoon," she finished, her head dropping on to his shoulder. "Our special song . . ."

The lights suddenly dimmed and, as if on cue, the bandleader announced the last number of 1945.

"Gentlemen, take your partners for a special song that means so much to so many. *Moonlight Becomes You* . . ."

ABOUT THE AUTHOR
"My parents inspired this story. When Dad got leave in late 1945, they headed to the ballroom where the coloured fountain was finally working again."

Bright IDEAS!

Share your top tips and we can all save some time…

Prevent slips

Tighten Your Grip

If you have difficulty opening bottles or jars, try wearing an ordinary household rubber glove. The glove allows you to get a better grip on the lid and prevents any injuries arising from slippery hands.
Patricia Taylor, Innerleithen

Wash And Go

Pop a bar of soap into the little mesh bag that comes with washing powder tablets and hang it on your garden tap. Now you can wash your dirty hands after gardening without having to go indoors and make a mess.
Stephen Newton, Spennymoor

Clean up outside

Brilliant Bird Food

Disposing of fat from the frying pan can be a messy business. I crumble bread into the hot fat and throw it to the birds when it has cooled. The birds love it – especially during the colder months – and the pan can simply be wiped clean.
Kathryn Truepenny, Southampton

The bread cleans the pan

Storage Solution

I keep a hold of the plastic containers that vegetables are often packaged in. They make ideal storage trays for various bits and bobs. I've used this one for my pencils, but they are also handy for storing keys, loose change and important receipts.
Tracey Griffin, Bristol

Everything in its place

The Little Silver Tree

Change is always difficult and Emily and her mum were facing big changes in their lives this Christmas…

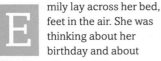

By Margaret Corbin

Emily lay across her bed, feet in the air. She was thinking about her birthday and about Christmas. She would be seven years old on the same day Jesus was born. She wondered if Jesus would have a party but she supposed if you were more than 2,000 years old you probably wouldn't really want to have one anyway.

Her party was going to be the Sunday before Christmas. She had asked Fiona, who was her very best friend, and Hannah and Abby to come. Jessica was horrible to her last week so she wouldn't be coming. This would be the first time Emily had had a proper birthday party. She was more excited about that than Christmas really, although she liked Christmas.

It sparkled and shimmered

her candle, and she loved the baby, so small, wrapped in a blanket, lying on straw. He had very blue eyes and didn't move at all.

The shepherds didn't move either. They had striped cloths on their heads and looked serious. They had sticks to lean on. It couldn't have been nice to be born in a manger, Emily thought. She knew she was born in the big

Emily really loved the Crib Service at the Church

Hospital, where there were proper rooms and beds and everything.

She sighed, thinking about poor Jesus, but he had presents too. Three Kings came and gave him gold, myrrh and frankinscense. She didn't know what the last two were but she knew about gold because her mum had a gold bracelet.

She told Emily, "Your dad gave me this when you were born because you were so precious." She'd hugged Emily who felt very safe knowing her dad had loved her so very much.

She specially liked the Crib Service at the Church where her school belonged. She liked the candles and the green holly and branches. It was cosy and friendly. She always went with her mum.

Michael, the Vicar, was nice and he told them how old Jesus was. Emily felt close to Jesus because they were both born on the very same day. At the Crib Service she liked walking to the manger with

She heard the sound of voices and got off the bed, padded across the room and opened the door. Oh dear, her mum and Richard were quarrelling. Emily **Continued overleaf…**

Continued from previous page

did wish they wouldn't. She shook her head with its dark curls, and her brown eyes clouded over.

She liked Richard, she really did. She didn't want him to die like her dad did, or go away. It was Richard who said she would be having a proper birthday party. Her mum had been a real grouch lately. She was tired and grumpy sometimes, not a bit like she usually was, loving and cuddly.

"I don't want a proper Christmas tree as you call it." Her mum sounded cross. "We've always had the little silver tree." Her voice seemed to tremble.

Emily remembered her mum telling her, "Your dad and I bought this tree our first Christmas. We didn't have enough money for a proper tree and it was in a sale." She laughed. "Nobody else wanted it."

Emily loved it. The leaves were upright and shiny, with decorations hanging from some of the branches. There was Father Christmas, a snowman, a wreath and an angel. Emily liked the angel best, she was there for the birthday, Emily was sure of that. She wished the silver tree could have lights, but it had always been special.

She and her mum had gone to Grandma's for Christmas and they took the silver tree with them. Christmas presents were under the tree and the birthday ones were on the sideboard. Emily's birthday

was always after dinner. It seemed a long time to wait.

There was always a special cake for her but the birthday presents came in the afternoon. The morning was for the stocking, with presents from the silver tree straight after breakfast. After the turkey dinner was the birthday. Emily wished her presents could be under the silver tree as well.

Her mum whispered, "Grandma always has Christmas presents after breakfast, we did it that way when I was a little girl."

Emily thought in wonder about her mum being a little girl. It was funny and she wondered if her mum was a happy little girl.

"It can be your birthday after that," Mum said and she stroked Emily's hair. "Grandma has been so good to us. Anyway, it's our silver tree, yours and mine."

Emily hugged her mum. Oh she was so lovely.

Every year since she could remember, when Emily first woke up on Christmas Day she wished Jesus a Happy Birthday, and then herself. She would open her Christmas stocking in bed with her mum and then they would go downstairs to Grandma's flat. They weren't going there this year, Richard said they were staying home. "Is that all right with you, love? Your mum can go to Mark's house." That was Mum's big brother, Uncle Mark. Her mum had nodded, eyes bright. She always seemed happy then.

Now they were quarrelling.

"I don't want a proper tree, as you call it." Her voice was different, all cold. "I just want the

ready to smile. Usually her mum would smile back and laugh, saying "Oh you," and give him a little push. Not today though. Her mum's voice was icy, like when she talked to the Headmaster at school about Emily being nearly left behind on the school outing.

Emily hugged her arms to her chest, she so didn't want Richard to go away. She didn't remember her dad but she had a picture of him in her room. Richard said she should always keep it and remember him, but he would be her second dad if she liked. She said a little prayer to God, "Please let them stop. I'll have Jessica to my birthday party if they stop. I promise."

The next night Richard brought

Emily felt like a real princess making the Christmas tree light up

silver tree, it was all we could afford… I like things the same."

There was silence and Emily strained to hear. She hoped they could keep the silver tree. She crept to the top of the stairs and sat down on the top step.

"Things aren't the same though, are they? I'm here now and I've always had a proper tree. I would really like one this year." Richard sounded quite angry.

Another silence and Emily could imagine his eyebrows raised and mouth turning up at the corners,

home a huge Christmas tree. He didn't use his key to come in but rang the bell instead.

When Mum went to the door, he said, "Good evening, do Susie and Emily live here?"

Emily came up behind her mum, who sounded only half cross. "Oh Richard, what are you playing at?"

"Special delivery for you, madam." He reached down and lifted the tree. It was taller than him and Emily felt a tingle of excitement. She wanted to jump up **Continued overleaf…**

and down and her eyes opened wide. It was green and smelt just like the big jar of pine salts, only better. There were lots and lots of lovely thick branches which glistened in the light of the porch.

Her mum seemed speechless and Richard quickly leaned down and kissed them both. "We will be known forever as the family with two Christmas trees, a green one and a silver one."

Emily knew then it would be all right. The green one was put in the lounge. It stood in the corner and Emily and her mum went shopping for decorations for it.

The three of them had a lovely time fixing it up, and it had candle lights on it as well. When it was time to switch them on Richard said, "Now we have a special

burst. Her mum and Richard came in to say goodnight and Emily drifted off to sleep thinking, "I will ask Jessica to my birthday party."

The party was a great success. There were sausages on sticks, pizza, cheese straws. Grandma came over for the party. She made a cake with silver balls and seven candles.

Grandad and Richard did a clown act which made them all laugh and at the very end Jessica said, "Thank you for asking me Emily, it was lovely."

That was good, Emily thought, Jessica was her friend as well now.

In a few days it would be Christmas and her proper birthday, and Jesus'. The green tree looked lovely, all shimmering and lit up with lights and silver stars and right on top was a fairy, dressed in

There, under the silver Christmas tree, were all Emily's birthday presents

person to turn on the lights for us. Will Emily step forward and do the honours please?"

With a flourish he urged her towards the switch and Emily felt like a real Princess making the tree light up. It was magical and she sighed with happiness, specially as Richard was kissing her mum under the mistletoe.

Emily was so excited when she went to bed she felt she could

gold and white, holding out a wand. She had a nice face.

Emily couldn't get to sleep on Christmas Eve and she heard their voices. She padded over to the door and opened it a little, then she got back into bed.

"The tree does look good Richard." Her mum's voice was soft.

"We're a family now, not just the two of you, there are three of us,

soon to be four. Life changes and we must change with it."

"I wonder who else is coming?" thought Emily drowsily, and then there was silence.

She woke at half-past five, sat up and first of all said Happy Birthday to herself and Jesus. He was old now but in the Church he was still a baby lying in the straw with the angels and shepherds looking after him. She liked that feeling.

Emily rubbed her eyes and reached for her stocking. It was all knobbly and exciting, different shapes, and there was a big orange and some sweets in the toe. They were always there. She was nearly at the end when her mum and Richard came into her room.

"Happy birthday," they both said and helped her finish the stocking.

Downstairs they switched on the lights on the green tree. Richard put an arm round both of them and said, "What did I tell you? Looks great, doesn't it?"

He sounded very happy and her mum pushed him and said "Oh you," and Emily knew that everything was fine.

Before they could look at the presents he said, "Come on then, into the dining room."

What a surprise – there under the silver tree, were all her birthday presents. The tree had lights, tiny stars, all shining bright. Emily caught her breath, she could hardly believe it.

"We do these first," said Richard, and Mum laughed.

"Oh yes." Her mum was smiling.

"Different pattern now, my love, your birthday is first. And we have another present as well."

Richard's face was all lit up. "Next year there will be four of us. You'll have a brother or sister to share as well."

Emily was quite dizzy with happiness. A baby, what about that? She just knew it would be a baby boy – just like Jesus. This was his special day too.

ABOUT THE AUTHOR

Margaret also has a Christmas birthday and, as a child it could seem overshadowed. Emily, a child of today, likes tradition but needs her own birthday too

Happy New

By Valerie Cannon

The dark night was serenely beautiful, with a faint wash of colour. The evening sky was clear, deep and soft-looking as silk velvet, black with just a faint hint of the deepest blue.

The moon shone palely yellow and had a wisp of a hazy veil around it. The stars stabbed little points of silvery light, scattered randomly over the whole expanse.

It was eleven o'clock on New Year's Eve.

Helen gazed upward and felt silent tears of despair run down her face. She should be with David.

The kiss would change slowly from tender love, through aching need, to passion; and he would pick her up and carry her indoors.

Memories. David's hands. David's touch. David's kiss. And most of all David's perfect love! The love she'd taken for granted.

But she was here now with Mark. Not David.

Oh, David. She loved him so much. Why had she sent him away? Why did they she say all those terrible things to him?

She couldn't even remember what the final row was about, so it couldn't have been that important. How could it have had such a devastating effect?

Mark was sweet and affectionate but she still missed David so much

They should be here together, standing side by side, hand in hand, marvelling at the serenity in the sky above them.

Together, they should be waiting for the distant sound of clocks striking midnight and the first firework to break the spell; and to share their first kiss of the year.

Helen shivered. It was cold out on the patio. She heard Mark's call and turned to go back inside, wiping her face with chilly hands. She didn't want Mark to see she was upset. She took a moment to compose herself before going upstairs to the bedroom.

Continued overleaf...

Year...

Enjoy our touching
story of love lost
but not forgotten

They should be
here together

Continued from previous page

Last year they had been at a party, she and David. They had been with a crowd of friends, dancing and laughing. They had had such glorious fun together. They did mad, wonderful things, especially at New Year.

In London they had splashed in the fountains of Trafalgar Square with everyone else.

They had partied all night and spent New Year's Day totally exhausted, with the gang, talking, laughing and reliving the excitement of the night before.

But, somehow, last year that had changed so much.

As midnight approached, she and David had felt the need to go outside quietly together, away from the noisy crowd – away from the boisterous hugging and kissing of everyone at midnight.

They had wanted only each other. And they had exchanged kisses that were deeper, more intense than anything before. They had spoken of lasting love, a shared future, made promises and commitments; and forged a new beginning together with new values and goals.

They had thought they were grown-up. How could they have been so wrong? How very stupid it all seemed now. All those resolutions had been thrown aside in silly, childish rows. How weak the commitment had really been.

Mark stirred beside her. He had fallen asleep, contented, his head on her shoulder.

Was it the New Year yet? Helen had lost track of time. Even with Mark beside her she couldn't forget about David. Easing herself out of bed, careful not to rouse him, she dressed quickly.

Helen felt hot, stinging tears welling up in her eyes again.

Mark was sweet and affectionate and she loved him with all her heart; but she still missed David. David was her rock, her support, her other half.

No one could take that place; he was a part of her now and nothing

It was five to twelve

and no one could change that.

Why hadn't she realised? Oh, they hadn't been ready for the reality of marriage.

They'd thought it would be pink and gold and bubbly and glowing with unblemished happiness all the time.

when she heard the soft noise behind her. She whirled around, her heart thumping wildly.

"Helen!" His voice was low.

She stared, confused, her arms wrapped around her waist in a defensive pose. In the semi-darkness it looked like David. It

"I love you. I never stopped loving you," he told her gently

They hadn't been prepared for the hard work that was involved in keeping a healthy marriage alive. But that was no reason to give in as soon as the bubbles went flat. She knew that now.

How could she have just told him to go? How could she ever have imagined she could manage to live without him?

If only she had a means of contacting David she would have done so; phoned immediately, even though it was so late. She missed him so very much.

She would apologise for whatever she had done. They could make another new start! But this time it would be better, stronger, and she would never let it go again because she knew now what life was like without him.

Helen hadn't missed the New Year, after all. It was five to twelve. Five minutes to go.

She was on the patio again, shivering but not realising it,

sounded like David. Had she simply conjured him up in her moment of desperate need?

He put out his hand and touched her arm gently. She felt the slight pressure. This was no figment of her imagination.

"Helen?" he said again, this time questioningly. He sounded uncertain, concerned and afraid.

"David?" She put out a hand to grasp his tightly.

There were no more doubts.

"I love you. I never stopped loving you," he told her.

He looked into her eyes with hope and trepidation.

"Oh, David, I…" She couldn't say anything else. Tears simply blocked everything.

He came to her and put his arms round her, tentatively at first, but stronger and tighter as she pressed into his chest, and buried her face in his neck to cry in earnest.

Midnight struck and in the
Continued overleaf…

Continued from previous page

distance a rocket whooshed into the air – but they didn't notice.

They held each other very tightly, neither wanting to be the first to break away.

"Let's get you inside, darling. You're freezing," David whispered in her ear eventually.

"Mark's asleep upstairs."

"Then I'd better go and see him," David said softly.

She followed him slowly upstairs, smiling.

When she got to the bedroom door he reached out his arm to gather her to his side.

They gazed down at Mark, arms

"I thought you might be out celebrating – with someone else perhaps"

Helen sighed. "I missed you so much. I'm so sorry I told you to go… I didn't mean it…I didn't know how to find you…"

David's mouth twisted.

"I was stupid to go. I knew what a strain you'd… we'd… been under – a difficult pregnancy, a new baby, sleepless nights. I should have understood… or tried to."

They stared at each other. He stroked her cheek gently.

"I won't go again," David assured. "I love you too much."

She smiled and turned her face into his caress. "I love you, too." Still wrapped in each other's arms, they went indoors.

Inside, he turned to face her.

"I thought you might be out, celebrating… with someone else." He was still uneasy, a little unsure of her feelings.

Helen smiled and shook her head. The smile that only lovers could give each other.

around each other. He opened his eyes suddenly, chuckled wetly and waved his chubby little baby fist around in the air.

They smiled back at him; Mark, their baby son.

David reached out to give him a finger to clutch. "Hi, Mark. Happy New Year. Daddy's home!"

Mark gurgled happily. Helen and David's eyes met, full of love, and they relaxed, suddenly sure of each other once more.

They were celebrating the New Year as a family. And determined to stay that way.

LOVED THIS STORY…

Look out for more touching stories in My Weekly, your favourite magazine, on sale every Thursday

Relax with *My Weekly*

Celebrities and inspirational women you'll love to read about

Travel to places you want to see

Health stories important to you

Delicious **recipes** you can't wait to make

Plus Big-name novelists, super short stories, mini-serials, puzzles, unusual facts and helpful tips

My Weekly

On Sale Every Thursday